SAQ® FOOTBALL
2nd edition

ALAN PEARSON

SPEED, AGILITY AND QUICKNESS FOR FOOTBALL

Contents

Acknowledgements iv

Forewords. v

Introduction vii

1 Dynamic Flex™ — Warm-up on the move
How Dynamic Flex™ differs from more traditional approaches, and how to design a warm-up around this. 1

2 Mechanics of Movement — The development of running form for football
The development and maintenance of football-specific running techniques (e.g. backward to lateral for a defender etc.), including co-ordination, balance, reaction and response 30

3 Innervation — Fast feet, agility, co-ordination, dynamic balance and control for football 70

4 Accumulation of Potential — Bringing together all previous components in an SAQ Football circuit 87

5 Explosion — Three-step, multi-directional acceleration for football. 96

6 Expression of Potential — Short competitive team games that prepare players for the next level of training 120

7 Vision and Reaction — Developing visual ability for football 126

8 Balance, Co-ordination, Feel and Judgement — The development of balance, co-ordination and body awareness 135

9 Position-specific Patterns of Movement — The development of multi-directional and explosive speed in a football-specific context including resisted, assisted, overspeed, vertical and horizontal power development techniques. 140

10 Warm-down and Recovery — Dynamic Flex™ drills to improve suppleness and dynamic range of movement in order to maximise recovery and improve training performance. 161

11 The SAQ Football Programme — Planning and integrating SAQ Training into a football-specific programme. 169

References 197

Glossary 199

Index of drills 201

Acknowledgements

This second edition of *SAQ Football* provides a clear example of what can be achieved when working with professional, motivated, forward-thinking people. The book has made great advances from the first edition due to this factor. I would like to thank the influences of John Green, Peter Friar, Neil Lewis, Glenn Roeder, Mick McCarthy, Kevin Ball, Paul Fairclough and also great players who constantly provided me with feedback and encouragement. Players such as David James, Steve Lomas, Christian Dailly, Don Hutchinson, Steve Palmer, Raimond van der Gow, Gary Breen plus many others.

A very special thank you to all SAQ Trainers and staff including David Hawkins, Marc Finney, Sarah Naylor, Angus Nicol, Brian Benjamin, Amanda Baker, Mike Callow, Steve Gilbert. A big thank you to Barnet FC, Sunderland AFC, West Ham Utd FC. Last but not least thanks and dedicated love to my wonderful wife, Silvana, without whose support this book would not have been possible.

Alan Pearson
2007

Alan and the publishers would also like to give special thanks to Barnet Football Club for their help with the photography. In particular, thanks go to the players and coaching staff from the Under 19s: Timothy Zobbo, James Cole, Lawrence Constanti, Vincent Freeman, Gianluca Pallodino, Joseph Tabiri, and Tim Trebes.

Forewords

Having seen Alan Pearson at work and having had the good fortune to listen to his invariably lucid and perceptive information on mobility, fitness and conditioning, I am pleased to note that he has now committed his thoughts to print. *SAQ Football* will be a most useful resource for technicians in the game and will, I feel sure, have an undoubted impact on the overall fitness of players, from top international professionals to those indulging in the great game of football as a recreational activity. Alan Pearson's well tried and carefully thought out theories are to be commended.

Craig Brown
National Coach and Technical Director,
Scottish Football Association

Having been a professional player for over 20 years I have seen many trainers and many training programmes – years of old school, prosaic programmes. My experience with Big Al (Alan Pearson) and SAQ fundamentally changed the way I looked at my training. The SAQ Programme is without doubt one of the reasons I still maintain my current position in the Premier League at nearly 37 years old. With continued use, I feel able to continue my career well into my 40s.

David James
Aston Villa, Liverpool, West Ham, Manchester
City, Portsmouth, England

As a Chartered Physiotherapist and Sports Scientist my job in professional football is to oversee injury prevention strategies, post-injury rehabilitation and the fitness conditioning of my players.

The 'fundamental skills and movement' taught through SAQ-based drills underpin all these goals and provide a framework upon which players can condition themselves to play their chosen sport. Consequently, I have actively promoted and utilised the SAQ principles in my work from junior football players to Premier League and International players.

In Alan Pearson, SAQ have somebody with unequalled enthusiasm and foresight to think 'outside the box' to ensure that the principles of SAQ underpin the fundamental movements of all sports, in a sports-specific manner.

I highly recommend *SAQ Football* as a resource tool but once you have an in-depth knowledge of the principles of SAQ training, the greatest resource tool is your imagination and your understanding of SAQ principles allied to your chosen sport.

Peter Friar MSc MCSP BSc (Hons)
Head of Sport Medicine, Sunderland AFC

In the modern game of football, explosive pace and the ability to change direction quickly and accelerate instantly are of increasing importance. I believe that the practices of SAQ Training implemented within a football programme over a period of time have a major impact on these areas. The ideas and functional exercises and drills developed within the SAQ Programme contribute to gaining the edge in a game where feet and inches can make all the difference between winning and losing.

Steve Palmer
Watford FC

The inspirational Alan Pearson and the SAQ programme have played a huge part in my development as a football coach and in working with players of all ages and abilities. This is unlike any other programme as it combines the technical and tactical aspects of sport with the physical and conditioning elements. As a professional player with Perth Glory in the Hyundai A-League (Australia), Alan's individual programme enabled me to compete at the highest level. I would recommend SAQ to all coaches and players no matter what age or ability.

Mark Lee
Perth Glory, Hyundai A League Australia,
Youth Development Officer,
Football West Perth, Australia

Having used SAQ as a player, I realised the benefits of the programme in both my training and match performances. Now I am a coach, I include the SAQ programme in training because it is fun, versatile and, above all, produces results.

Kevin Ball Assistant Academy Director,
Sunderland AFC

The high level rehabilitation of elite athletes that I am involved with is guided by the main principles of SAQ. It is important to accept that this approach to sports people is NOT just a series of exercises, but a progressive programme. Some conditioning approaches come and go, but the SAQ way is the correct way to work! This stuff really works!

John Green Bsc Hon, MCSP, HPC
Premiership Physiotherapist and Sports
Scientist. Rehabilitation expert to premiership
stars including Kieran Dyer, Michael Owen and
Dean Ashton.

Introduction

Football is possibly the most popular and most widely played sport in the world and is enjoyed by players of all ages, male, female, professional and amateur. The game also commands a larger spectator base than any other sport on the planet.

There is nothing more exhilarating than a player who explodes through a defensive gap, checks, turns and side-steps to avoid desperate, defensive lunges and fires the ball home. Or a centre-half who defies gravity by jumping into the air, hanging there long enough to intercept a crossed ball with his head before redirecting it to a supporting midfielder's feet for a swift and decisive counter-attack. The incredible explosive, athletic ability of a goalkeeper diving at full stretch to deflect a shot around the post is an awesome sight.

These wonderful acts of speed, agility and quickness make the difference between winning and losing. Often thought to be a 'God-given' gift and therefore neglected on the training field, these skills are admired and believed to be essential for success within the game by players, managers, coaches and trainers.

The SAQ Programme for Football is the first ever football-specific programme designed to develop these key skills. The programme also has other significant benefits such as improving eye, hand and foot co-ordination, strength, explosive power and core control, as well as being full of variety and great fun. The secret lies in the SAQ Continuum and the use of progressive sequential learning techniques, breaking down complex sports science and making it easy to understand and practical to use. The end result is the development of multi-directional explosive speed specifically for football. This unique programme can be adapted to meet the needs both of squad training and of individual players who require position-specific development. The Programme provides an ideal opportunity for children as young as six up to and including the most senior of professional players to learn and improve.

The Programme has evolved from years of practical experience out on the training fields of world football, talking to World Cup coaches, Premiership managers, elite and amateur players through to little league players and school kids. This is what makes it so unique and in demand throughout the world. Many of Europe's top clubs now include SAQ Training in their everyday sessions as it adds a new dimension to their preparation and also produces demonstrable results on the playing field.

This book allows coaches, trainers, managers and players to understand how and why SAQ Programmes work. It provides clear, precise examples of how to put the theory into practice on the training ground. Its progressive structure even covers advanced position-specific drills that will allow you to integrate SAQ Training into all of your football training sessions.

What is SAQ Training?

Speed has long been considered as just one single entity, that is how fast an object can go from point A to point B. Only recently has speed been studied and broken down into stages such as acceleration, the 'planing out' phase, deceleration, and so on. Much of this research has been carried out by sports coaches involved in straight-line running, with the result that the jumping, turning and zigzagging speed necessary in football has been somewhat neglected.

Those involved in the development of SAQ Programmes have sought to fill this void in order to develop all types of speed, particularly for team sports such as football. SAQ Programmes break speed down into three main areas of skill: speed, agility and quickness. Although these may appear to be quite similar, they are in fact very different in terms of how they need to be trained, developed and integrated into a player's performance. When these skills are successfully combined and specialist SAQ Equipment is utilised, they provide coaches with the tools they need to make a good player into an outstanding player. It is remarkable what players can achieve with an SAQ Programme.

SPEED

A crucial part of any player's game is the ability to cover the ground efficiently and economically over the first few metres and then to open up stride length and increase stride frequency when working over 35 to 45 metres. Speed means the maximum velocity a player can achieve and maintain. Most humans can maintain this maximum velocity only for a short period of time and distance. Speed can also be measured by the amount of time it takes a player to cover a particular distance.

Training to improve maximum speed requires a great deal of focus on correct running mechanics, stride length and frequency, the leg cycle and hip height/position. Drills such as the 'dead-leg run' and stride frequency drills that help to develop an economical running technique can all be easily integrated into a training session.

The best sprinters spend very little time in contact with the ground, and any contact they do make is extremely efficient and powerful. Focusing on the mechanics of running helps to control this power and use it efficiently and sparingly. Training when fresh is also crucial in order for a player to attain his maximum speed. Many sprinters can reproduce top speeds only for a few weeks of the year, but practising correct running mechanics on the training field will benefit players of the game greatly. How often have you seen a footballer run as if they are playing a kettledrum, that is with poor arm mechanics? Running like this will have a detrimental effect on the overall running technique and, more importantly, the speed of the player.

AGILITY

Agility is the ability to change direction without losing balance, strength, speed or body control. There is a direct link between improved agility and the development of an individual's timing, rhythm and movement.

Agility training ensures that a player develops the best offensive and defensive skills possible with the greatest quickness, speed and control and the least amount of wasted energy and movement. Agility also has many other benefits, including helping to prevent niggling injuries and teaching the muscles how to fire properly and control minute shifts in ankle, knee, hip, back, shoulder and neck joints for optimum body alignment.

Another very important benefit is that agility training is long lasting. Unlike speed, stamina and weight training, it does not have to be maintained in order to retain the benefits. Consider the elderly person who can still ride a bicycle 40 years after having last ridden one. Agility training acts like an indelible mark, programming muscle memory.

There are four elements to agility

- balance
- co-ordination
- programmed agility
- random agility.

Each of these elements requires speed, strength, timing and rhythm.

Balance

Balance is a foundation of athleticism. Players learn balance by focusing on their centre of gravity while standing, stopping and walking; this can be taught and retained relatively quickly. Examples include standing on one leg, walking on a balance beam, standing on a balance beam, standing on an agility disc, walking backwards with your eyes closed and jumping on a mini-trampoline and then freezing. Balance training requires only a couple of minutes, two or three times a week, early in the morning and early in a training session. However, balance is complicated by the other elements of agility.

Co-ordination

Co-ordination training challenges players to master simple skills under more difficult stresses. Co-ordination work is often slow and methodical with an emphasis on correct biomechanics during athletically demanding movements. Co-ordination can be trained by breaking a skill down into sections, then gradually bringing those sections back together. Co-ordination activities include footwork drills, tumbling, rolling and jumping. More difficult examples are walking on a balance beam while playing catch, running along a line while a partner lightly pulls and pushes in an attempt to move the player off the line and jumping on and off an agility disc while holding a jelly ball.

Programmed agility

'Programmed' agility is when a player has already experienced the skill or stress that is to be placed on him/her and is aware of the pattern and sequence of demands of that experience. In short, the player has already been programmed. Programmed agility drills can be conducted at high speeds, but must first be learned at low, controlled speeds. Examples include zigzag marker spot/cone drills, shuttle runs and 'T' marker spot/cone drills, all of which involve changes of direction along a known, standardised pattern. There is no spontaneity. Once these types of drills have been learned and performed on a regular basis, times and performances will improve and advances in strength, explosion, flexibility and body control will be witnessed. This is true of players of any ability.

Random agility

The final element of agility – and the most difficult to master, prepare for and perform – is 'random' agility. Here, the player performs tasks with unknown patterns and unknown demands. The coach can incorporate visual and audible reactive skills so that the player has to make split-second decisions with movements based upon the various stimuli. The skill level is much closer to actual game-like situations. Random agility can be trained by games like tag, read and react (tennis ball drops and dodge), dodge ball and more specific training such as jumping and landing followed by an immediate unknown movement demand from the coach.

Agility training is challenging, fun and exciting. There is the opportunity for tremendous variety and training should not become boring or laborious. Agility is not just for those with elite sporting abilities: try navigating through a busy shopping mall!

QUICKNESS

When a player accelerates, a great deal of force has to be generated and transferred through the foot to the ground. This action is similar to rolling a towel up (the 'leg'), holding one end in your hand and flicking it out to achieve the 'cracking' noise from the other end (the 'foot'). Acceleration occurs in a fraction of a second and takes the body from a static position to motion. Muscles actually lengthen and then shorten instantaneously; that is, an 'eccentric' followed by a 'concentric' contraction. This process is known as the stretch-shortening cycle (SCC). SAQ Training concentrates on improving the neuromuscular system that impacts on this process, so that this initial movement – whether lateral, linear or vertical – is automatic, explosive and precise. The reaction time is the time it takes for the brain to receive and respond to a stimulus by sending a message to the muscle, causing it to contract. This helps a player to cut right–left–right and then burn down the sideline, or the goalkeeper to make a split-second save. Ongoing SAQ Training reprograms the neuromuscular system and removes restrictive mental blocks and thresholds. As a consequence, messages from the brain have a clear path to the muscles, resulting in an instinctively quicker player.

Quickness training begins with 'innervation' (isolated fast contractions of an individual joint). Examples include repeating the same explosive movement over a short period of time, such as fast feet and line drills. These quick, repetitive motions take the body through the gears, moving it in a co-ordinated manner to develop speed. Integrating quickness training into the programme throughout the year by using fast feet and reaction drills will result in the muscles having increased firing rates. This means that players will be capable of faster, more controlled acceleration. The goal is to ensure that your players explode over the first 3–5 metres. Imagine that the firing between the nervous system and the muscles are the gears in a car; the timing, speed and smoothness of the gear change means that the wheels and thus the car accelerate away efficiently with balance and co-ordination, so that the wheels do not spin and the car does not lose control.

Movement skills

Many elements of balance and co-ordination involve the processing of sensory information from within the body. Proprioceptors are sensors that detect muscular tension, tension in tendons, relative tension and pressure in the skin. In addition, the body has a range of other sensors that detect balance. The ability to express balance and co-ordination is highly dependent on the effectiveness of the body's internal sensors and proprioceptors, just like the suspension on a car. Through training, these sensors, and the neural communication system within the body, become more effective. In addition, the brain becomes more able to interpret these messages and formulate the appropriate movement response. This physiological development underpins effective movement and future movement skill development.

Fundamental Skills

In today's society, many children do not experience appropriate movement opportunities necessary for the development of basic movement abilities (Walkley et al., 1993). It is vital that children experience the full range of the skills listed in the table below (Sugden et al., 1998) if they are going to become competent football players in the future.

Fundamental movement skills		
Stability	**Locomotion**	**Manipulation**
Bending	Walking	Throwing
Stretching	Running	Catching
Twisting	Jumping	Kicking
Turning	Hopping	Trapping
Swinging	Skipping	Striking
Inverted supports	Galloping	Volleying
Body rolling	Sliding	Bouncing
Landing/stopping	Leaping	Ball rolling
Dodging	Climbing	Punting

Source: Gallahue and Donnelly, 2003
From *Development PE for All Children* by David L Gallahue and F Cleland Donnelly

Rehabilitation: injury prevention

The SAQ Programme has been used successfully at all levels of the game by leading physiotherapists during player rehabilitation. Reports from trainers and coaches also indicate that injury levels have dropped dramatically after implementing the programme. A Premiership club's Injury Report Audit from the 2005–2006 season highlights that, before SAQ Training was introduced in late November/early December, days off due to injury in the senior squad was 350 – 150 days above the national average for that month. After the introduction of SAQ, this was reduced over a 14-week period to 120 – 15 days below the February national average. This audit clearly indicates that when SAQ is implemented effectively within a football programme it can have a major impact on reducing injury levels among players.

Cardiovascular conditioning

The SAQ Programme is a tremendous tool for the development of cardiovascular fitness, which simulates the game-related intensity experienced by leading players. The heart rate of an international player at a premiership club was taken while working through an SAQ session that included a Dynamic Flex warm-up, agility drills (including fast feet ladders and hurdle work), one-on-one keep ball, viper belt resistance work plus recovery in between bouts of activity, and cool-down. Note the periods of low heart rate and high heart rate, which reflect the high-intensity, intermittent nature of match play. The player's heart rate average was 129 bpm, with a low of 78 bpm and a maximum of 190 bpm.

SAQ Equipment

SAQ Equipment adds variety and stimuli to your training session. Drill variations are endless and, once mastered, the results achieved can be quite astonishing. Players of all ages and abilities enjoy the challenges presented to them when training with SAQ Equipment, particularly when introduced in a football-specific manner.

When using SAQ Equipment, coaches, trainers and players must be aware of the safety issues involved and of the reduced effectiveness and potentially dangerous consequence of using unbranded/inferior equipment.

The following pages introduce a variety of SAQ Equipment recommended for use in many of the drills detailed later in this book.

FAST FOOT™ LADDERS

These are constructed of webbing with hard round plastic rungs spaced approximately 18 inches apart. They come in sets of four pieces, each measuring 7.5 feet. The pieces can be joined together or used as four separate ladders; they can also be folded over to create different angles on which players can perform drills. Fast Foot Ladders are great for improving agility and for the development of explosive fast feet.

MICRO & MACRO V HURDLES™

SAQ hurdles come in two sizes: Micro V Hurdles, measuring 18 cm and Macro V Hurdles, measuring 30 cm. They are constructed from hard plastic and have been specifically designed to be safe, free-standing pieces of equipment. It is recommended that the hurdles be used in sets of six to eight to perform the mechanics drills detailed later. They are ideal for practising running mechanics and low-impact plyometrics. The micro hurdles are also great for lateral work.

SONIC CHUTE™

These are constructed from webbing (the belt), nylon cord and a lightweight cloth 'chute', the size of which can vary from 1.5 to 2 metres. The belts have a release mechanism that, when pulled, drops the chute so that the player can explode forwards. These are great for developing sprint endurance.

VIPER BELT™

This is a resistance belt specially made for high-intensity training. It has three stainless steel anchor points where a flexi-cord can be attached. The flexi-cord is made from surgical tubing with a specific elongation. The Viper Belt has a safety belt and safety fasteners, is double-stitched and provides a great level of resistance. This piece of equipment is great for developing explosive speed in all directions.

SIDE-STEPPERS™

These are padded ankle straps that are connected by an adjustable flexi-cord. They are great for the development of lateral movements.

REACTOR™

A rubber ball specifically shaped so that it bounces in unpredictable directions.

OVERSPEED TOW ROPE™

This is made up of two belts and a 45-metre nylon cord pulley system. It can be used to provide resistance and is specifically designed for the development of express overspeed and swerve running.

BREAK-AWAY BELT™

These are webbing belts that are connected by Velcro-covered connecting strips. They are great for mirror drills and position-specific marking drills, breaking apart when one player gets away from the other.

STRIDE FREQUENCY CANES™

These are different coloured plastic canes measuring 1.2 metres that are used to mark out stride patterns.

SPRINT SLED™

This is a metal sled with a central area that can accommodate different weights and a running harness that is attached to the sled by webbing straps 7 – 9 metres long.

JELLY BALLS™

These are round soft rubber balls filled with a water-based 'jelly-like' substance. They come in different weights, from 2 to 8 kg. They differ from old-fashioned medicine balls because they can be bounced with great force onto hard surfaces.

HAND WEIGHTS™

These are foam-covered weights weighing between 0.5 and 1 kg. They are safe and easy to use both indoors and outdoors.

VISUAL ACUITY RING™

This is a hard plastic ring approximately 75 cm in diameter with four different coloured balls attached to it, equally distributed around the ring. The ring helps to develop visual acuity and tracking skills when thrown and caught between the players. This piece of equipment is particularly good for goalkeepers. (Patent pending.)

PERIPHERAL VISION STICK™

This is simple but very effective for training peripheral vision. It is approximately 1 metre long with a brightly coloured ball at one end. Once again, this is great for all players, but particularly for goalkeepers. (Patent pending.)

BUNT BAT™

This is a 1-metre-long stick with a coloured ball at each end and another in the middle. Working in pairs, one player holds the bat with two hands while the other throws a small ball or beanbag for that player to 'bunt' or fend off. Once again, this is great for the development of hand–eye co-ordination for all players, particularly goalkeepers.

AGILITY DISC™

This is an inflatable rubber disc 45 cm across. They are multi-purpose, but are particularly good for proprioceptive and core development work. Players can stand, kneel, sit or lie on the discs to perform all types of exercise.

SIDESTRIKE™

This is a heavy-duty platform with raised, angled ends for foot placement. The ends are adjustable to accommodate different sized athletes, and the surface is padded to provide protection. This is a fantastic piece of equipment for the development of explosive footwork and is ideal for football players.

MARKER SPOTS™

These are heavy-duty, non-slip marker spots and are ideal for most surfaces. They help to prevent players from slipping, which can happen with traditional cones. The spots are brightly coloured and therefore easily recognisable.

VISUAL ENHANCEMENT TRAINING (VET) GOGGLES™

These goggles use the latest visual training technology (pin-hole technology) to improve the eye's ability to focus on objects. They include a head-band, so they can be used in training situations. (Patent pending.)

SPIKED POLES™

These come in various colours and can be used to organise and mark out any training space safely, and are ideal for agility and pressing work.

MANNEQUINS™

These life-size mannequins can be used to simulate the position of opposition players. They are fantastic for training game-like situations.

The SAQ Continuum

Many games activities are characterised by explosive movements, acceleration and deceleration, agility, turning ability and speed of responses (Smythe, 2000). The SAQ Continuum is the sequence and progression of components that make up an SAQ Training session. The progressive elements include football-specific running patterns and drills, including ball work. The Continuum is also flexible and, once the pre-season foundation work has been completed, during the season when time and recovery are of the essence short combination SAQ Training sessions provide a constant top-up to the skills learned previously.

SAQ Training is like any other fitness training: if neglected, players' explosive multi-directional power will diminish. The component parts of the SAQ Continuum and how they relate to football are as follows:

- **Dynamic Flex™** – warm-up on the move.
- **Mechanics of movement** – the development of running form for football.
- **Innervation** – fast feet, agility and control for football.
- **Accumulation of potential** – bringing together the previous components in an SAQ Training football circuit.

- **Explosion** – the development of explosive three-step multi-directional acceleration for football.

- **Expression of potential** – short competitive team games that prepare players for the next level of training.

- **Warm down** – reverse Dynamic Flex.

Position-specific drills and skills can be implemented throughout the Continuum.

CHAPTER 1 DYNAMIC FLEX™

WARM-UP ON THE MOVE

It is common knowledge and practice that the body should be prepared before engaging in intense or strenuous exercise. The warm-up should achieve a change in a number of physiological responses in order that the body can work safely and effectively:

- increased body temperature, specifically core (deep) muscle temperature
- increased heart rate and blood flow
- increased breathing rate
- increased elasticity of muscular tissues
- activated mental alertness

The warm-up should take a player from a rested state to the physiological state required for participation in the session that is to follow. The warm-up should gradually increase in intensity. In addition, it should be fun and stimulating for the players, switching them on mentally.

In the past, standard training sessions would begin with players warming up by jogging around the pitch, then performing a series of static stretches with a focus on the main muscle groups in the body, then carrying out some ball work. However, static stretches are not only irrelevant within the game of football, but are actually likely to cause injury and loss of power (Kokkonen, Nelson and Cornwell, 1998). Footballers do not need to be able to do the splits like gymnasts and dancers, but they do need to be able to perform dynamic, explosive, multi-directional movements while giving and receiving the ball, performing side-on volleys and over-head kicks. Dynamic Flex allows players to do this: flexibility in action, if you like, combined with power, strength and control. You do not pull a muscle standing still, so how can you warm it up statically?

Indeed, research has shown that static stretching before training or competitions can actually be detrimental to performance: in research carried out by Rosenbaum and Hennig (1995), static stretching resulted in a 5 per cent reduction in peak force, an 8 per cent reduction in rate of force production and a decrease in Achilles tendon reflex activity; according to Oberg (1993), static stretching resulted in a decrease in torque during eccentric contractions; and according to Bennett (1999), pre-exercise static stretches decreased eccentric strength by 9 per cent for up to one hour. The eccentric strength of a muscle is its ability to apply force when lengthening, for example when a player lands then applies the breaks immediately after a defensive header. According to the research, his or her ability would typically be reduced by up to 9 per cent for up to an hour after static stretching. Sadly, we still see players performing static stretches not only before the start of the game but also during the game, including the reserves warming up on the sideline.

One of the main arguments in favour of static stretching has been that it helps to prevent injury and muscle soreness. Once again, scientific research suggests the opposite. Gleim and McHugh (1997) state that it is not possible to draw any relationship between flexibility and risk of injury. Pope (1999) concluded that there was no difference in occurrence of injury between army recruits who stretched and those who did not. Herbert and Gabriel (2002) suggest that stretching before exercising does not seem to confer a practically useful reduction in the risk of injury. Research into the effects of static stretching on Delayed Onset of Muscle Soreness (DOMS) is inconclusive, and limited: Smith et al (1993) reported that a group performing static stretching experienced higher levels of DOMS than a non-stretching group; according to Herbert and Gabriel (2002), 'stretching before or after exercise does not confer protection from muscle soreness'. Muscle soreness after physical activity is natural. After a period of continued activity, the body will adapt and cope with the soreness. McMillian, Moore, Hatler and Taylor (2005) compared the effects on power and agility of a dynamic warm-up with those of a static warm-up on 30 cadets in the United States Military Academy. Their results strongly confirm that the Dynamic Flex warm-up enhanced performance, while static stretching did not. Could you imagine a lion in the Serengeti stalking its antelope prey, stopping and performing static stretches before accelerating for the kill? It just doesn't make sense.

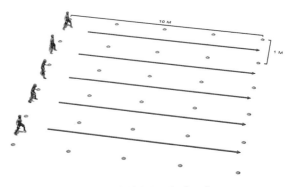

Figure 1.1(a) Standard grid

Pre-training and pre-game warm-up

It is important to differentiate between warming up for training and warming up for a game.

PRE-TRAINING WARM-UP

Here, dynamic flex can be used for 5–20 minutes and the warm-up can be integrated with combination work such as fast feet and mechanics, depending on the time you have allocated. This is also a great time to introduce football-specific concepts, focusing on improving a player's ability to perform Dynamic Flex, improve range of movement (ROM) and highlight the positives and negatives of the player's performance. The warm-up can be performed using different grid formations, which will help maintain motivation. Start with a standard grid measuring 18 x 18 metres (20 x 20 yards) (see figure 1.1(a)). Progress to other grid variations once the Dynamic Flex exercises have been mastered (see figures 1.1(b) to 1.1(e)). It is crucial to inform players why Dynamic Flex is being used and to explain the benefits of each particular drill.

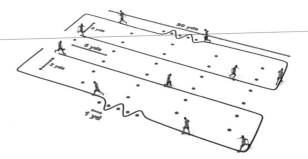

Figure 1.1(b) Grid variation

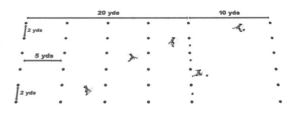

Figure 1.1(c) Split grid

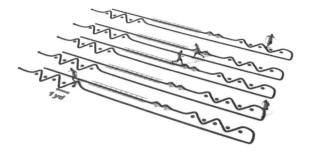

Figure 1.1(d) Combination warm-up grid 1

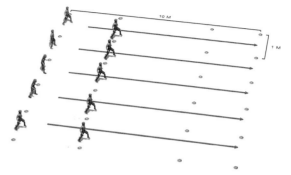

Figure 1.1(g) Two line out and back grid

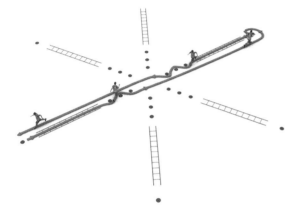

Figure 1.1(e) Combination warm-up grid 2 – multi-crossover

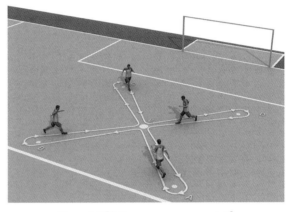

Figure 1.1(h) Four corner warm-up grid

PRE-GAME WARM-UP

Here, the focus must be on preparing players to be multi-directionally explosive immediately from the kick off. This is not the time to introduce a varied warm-up; keep to a simple, familiar structure so that the players' main focus is the game. The following pre-game warm-up for a 3:00 pm kick-off has been used successfully at Premiership level and is suitable for all levels of the game:

- 2:20–2:30 pm   Dynamic Flex warm-up
- 2:30–2:35 pm   Ball work in small groups
- 2:35–2:40 pm   Small sides game

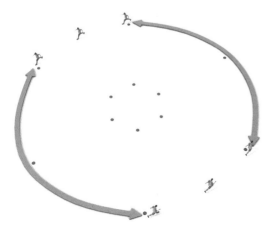

Figure 1.1(f) Circle grid

- 2:40–2:47 pm   Players' own time
- 2:47–2:50 pm   4–18-yard explosive crossing sprints
- 2:50 pm   Return to changing room

The walk or jog back to the changing room will take 2–3 minutes. By the time the players return to the changing room, there should be no longer than 6–7 minutes between the end of the warm-up and the start of the game; any longer and the players will begin to cool down. This pre-game warm-up has been developed so that players finish the warm-up explosively and therefore start the game explosively from the first kick.

Caution

I have recently observed a number of warm-ups that comprise a mixture of Dynamic Flex movements and static stretching. The argument of the trainers was that this provided the best of both worlds. However, any static stretching – irrespective of the use of dynamic movement patterns – is detrimental to performance prior to training and playing. There should be no static stretching whatsoever at this stage.

DRILL ARM ROLL AND JOG

Aim
To improve shoulder mobility, balance and co-ordination; to increase body temperature; to develop positive foot-to-ground contact.

Area/equipment
An indoor or outdoor grid 18 metres in length. The width of the grid is variable depending on the size of the squad.

Description
Players cover the length of the grid by jogging forwards and backwards, rolling their arms forwards so that they move from below the waist to above the head in a rolling motion.

Key teaching points
- The arms should be slightly bent
- Keep off the heels
- Maintain an upright posture
- Ensure there is adequate spacing between players

What you might see	Solution
■ Arms rotated horizontally	■ Brush the arms past the ears in a more vertical rotational movement
■ Sinking into the hips	■ Breathe in and out lightly, holding the contraction so that normal breathing can occur

Sets and reps
2 x 18 metres: 1 forwards and 1 backwards.

Variation/progression
Perform the drill laterally.

DRILL WALKING ON THE BALLS OF THE FEET

Aim
To stretch the shins and improve ankle mobility; to improve balance and co-ordination; to increase body temperature.

Area/equipment
An indoor or outdoor grid 18 metres in length. The width of the grid is variable depending on the size of the squad.

Description
Players cover the length of the grid by walking on the balls of the feet, then return to the start by repeating the drill moving backwards.

Key teaching points
- Do not walk on the toes
- Keep off the heels
- Maintain correct arm mechanics (see pages 45–47)
- Squeeze the buttocks together
- Maintain an upright posture

What you might see	Solution
Walking on the toes	Player should focus on walking on the balls of the feet, keeping the head horizontal with the body leaning slightly forwards
Legs too wide apart	Feet should be shoulder-width apart – use marker dots for spacing if necessary

Sets and reps
2 x 18 metres: 1 forwards and 1 backwards.

Variation/progression
Perform the drill with the arms stretched out above the head. This will challenge balance and core control.

DRILL   *JOG AND HUG*

Aim
To improve shoulder and chest mobility; to improve balance and co-ordination; to increase body temperature.

Area/equipment
An indoor or outdoor grid 18 metres in length. The width of the grid is variable depending on the size of the squad.

Description
Players cover the length of the grid by slowly jogging forwards, bringing the arms around the front of the body so that the fingers can grip behind the opposite shoulder. Alternate the arms over and under.

Key teaching points
■ Squeeze slowly
■ Jog on the balls of the feet
■ Maintain an upright posture
■ Ensure there is adequate spacing between players

What you might see   Solution
■ Trunk held too upright   ■ Player should tilt the trunk slightly forwards and drop the chin closer to the chest

■ Running on the heels   ■ Lean the body forwards – this will push the weight on to the balls of the feet

Sets and reps
2 x 18 metres: 1 forwards and 1 backwards.

Variation/progression
Squeeze and then rotate the core, turning from left to right, then right to left, and so on.

DRILL   *ANKLE FLICKS*

Aim
To stretch the calves and improve ankle mobility; to improve balance, co-ordination and rhythm of movement; to prepare for good foot-to-floor contact; to increase body temperature.

Area/equipment
An indoor or outdoor grid 18 metres in length. The width of the grid is variable depending on the size of the squad.

Description
Players cover the length of the grid in a skipping motion where the balls of the feet plant, then flick up towards the shin. The player should move in a rhythmic, bouncing manner. The player then returns to the start by repeating the drill backwards.

Key teaching points
- Work off the balls of the feet, not the toes
- Practise the first few steps on the spot before moving off
- Maintain correct arm mechanics (see pages 45–47)
- Maintain an upright posture

What you might see	Solution
■ Poor plantar/dorsiflex range of movement (raising and lowering of the toes)	■ Player can pull toes towards the shin on the upward flick
■ Jerky, un-rhythmic movement	■ Player can call 'up, down' or 'one, two' to help with rhythm

Sets and reps
2 x 18 metres: 1 forwards and 1 backwards.

Variation/progression
Perform the drill laterally.

DRILL SMALL SKIPS

Aim
To improve lower leg flexibility and ankle mobility; to improve balance, co-ordination and rhythm; to develop positive foot-to-ground contact; to increase body temperature.

Area/equipment
An indoor or outdoor grid 18 metres in length. The width of the grid is variable depending on the size of the squad.

Description
Players cover the length of the grid in a low skipping motion, then return to the start by repeating the drill backwards.

Key teaching points
- Raise the knees to an angle of about 45–55 degrees
- Work off the balls of the feet
- Maintain correct arm mechanics (see pages 45–47)
- Maintain an upright posture
- Maintain a good rhythm

What you might see
- Too high knee lift

- Poor rhythm

Solution
- Player to focus on the knee not coming any higher than the waistband
- Same as above

Sets and reps
2 x 18 metres: 1 forwards and 1 backwards.

Variation/progression
Perform the drill laterally.

DRILL   WIDE SKIPS

Aim
To improve hip and ankle mobility; to improve balance, co-ordination and rhythm; to increase body temperature.

Area/equipment
An indoor or outdoor grid 18 metres in length. The width of the grid is variable depending on the size of the squad.

Description
Players cover the length of the grid by skipping. The feet should remain wider than shoulder-width apart and the knees should face outwards at all times. The player then returns to the start by repeating the drill backwards.

Key teaching points
- Keep off the heels
- Maintain correct arm mechanics (see pages 45–47)
- Maintain an upright posture
- Do not take the thigh above a 90-degree angle

What you might see	Solution
Landing on flat feet	Player should lean slightly forwards – ask them to focus their eyes on an object 15–20 yards ahead on the floor
Arms and elbows held in too tight to the body	Encourage good arm drive – the inside of the wrist should brush the hips and the thumb should come up to the side of the face

Sets and reps
2 x 18 metres: 1 forwards and 1 backwards.

Variation/progression
Perform the drill laterally.

DRILL   *SINGLE-KNEE DEAD-LEG LIFT*

Aim
To improve buttock flexibility and hip mobility; to isolate the correct 'running cycle' motion for each leg.

Area/equipment
An indoor or outdoor grid 18 metres in length. The width of the grid is variable depending on the size of the squad.

Description
Players cover the length of the grid by quickly bringing the knee of one leg up to a 90-degree angle. The other leg should remain as straight as possible with a very short lift away from the ground throughout the movement. The ratio should be 1:4, i.e. one lift to every four steps. Work one leg on the way down the grid and the other on the return.

Key teaching points
■ Do not raise the knee above a 90-degree angle
■ Strike the floor with the ball of the foot
■ Keep the foot facing forwards
■ Maintain correct running mechanics (see pages 48–62)

What you might see	Solution
■ Both knees being lifted	■ Player should focus on one side only and perform the drill at a walking pace, i.e. walk, lift, walk, lift
■ Stuttering form and rhythm phase	■ Use marker dots to help rhythm and work on this drill in the mechanics
■ Knee lift angled either out or across the body	■ Player should perform the drill with the arm on the knee-lift side held out in front of them, the knee should be brought up to touch the hand

Sets and reps
2 x 18 metres: 1 forwards and 1 backwards.

Variation/progression
Vary the lift ratio, e.g. 1:2 (one lift to every two steps).

DRILL | *HIGH KNEE-LIFT SKIP*

Aim
To improve buttock flexibility and hip mobility; to increase range of motion (ROM) over a period of time; to develop rhythm; to increase body temperature.

Area/equipment
An indoor or outdoor grid 18 metres in length. The width of the grid is variable depending on the size of the squad.

Description
Players cover the length of the grid using a high skipping motion, then return to the start by repeating the drill backwards.

Key teaching points
- The thigh should be taken past 90 degrees
- Work off the balls of the feet
- Maintain a strong core
- Maintain an upright posture
- Control the head by looking forwards at all times
- Maintain correct arm mechanics (see pages 45–47)

What you might see
- Landing on the heels

- Inconsistency of knee lift (i.e. to different heights)

Solution
- Player should lean forwards and focus on the balls of the feet
- The knee should be raised to just above waist. Player should perform the drill at walking place so the range of movement can be practised

Sets and reps
2 x 18 metres: 1 forwards and 1 backwards.

Variation/progression
Perform the drill laterally.

DRILL KNEE-ACROSS SKIP

Aim
To improve outer hip flexibility and hip mobility over a period of time; to develop balance and co-ordination; to increase body temperature.

Area/equipment
An indoor or outdoor grid 18 metres in length. The width of the grid is variable depending on the size of the squad.

Description
Players cover the length of the grid in a skipping motion where the knee comes across the body, then returns to the start by repeating the drill backwards.

Key teaching points
- Do not force an increased ROM
- Work off the balls of the feet
- Maintain a strong core
- Maintain an upright posture
- Control the head by looking forwards at all times
- Use the arms primarily for balance

What you might see	Solution
■ Too high knee lift	■ Player to focus on the knee not coming any higher than the waistband
■ Skipping on the heels	■ Player should lean slightly forwards and transfer weight to the balls of the feet

Sets and reps
2 x 18 metres: 1 forwards and 1 backwards.

Variation/progression
Perform the drill laterally.

DRILL LATERAL RUNNING

Aim
To develop an economic knee drive; to stretch the side of the quadriceps; to prepare for an efficient lateral running technique; to increase body temperature.

Area/equipment
An indoor or outdoor grid 18 metres in length. The width of the grid is variable depending on the size of the squad.

Description
Players cover the length of the grid with short lateral steps, leading with the left or right shoulder, then return with the opposite shoulder leading.

Key teaching points
- Keep the hips square
- Work off the balls of the feet
- Do not skip
- Do not let the feet cross over
- Maintain an upright posture
- Do not sink into the hips or fold at the waist
- Do not over-stride – use short, sharp steps
- Maintain correct arm mechanics (see pages 45–47)

What you might see	Solution
Feet crossing or being brought together	Get player to focus on working with their feet shoulder-width apart. The ROM of the feet should be from just outside the shoulder to just inside the shoulder, using the outside of the foot as the gauge
Skipping sideways	Player should focus on a stepping rather than a skipping motion; use marker spots to indicate where the feet should be placed in lateral stepping
No arm movement or arms by the sides	Players should brush the side of their body with the side of their wrist and bring their hands up to the side of the face. This will help arm drive

Sets and reps
2 x 18 metres: 1 leading with the left shoulder and 1 leading with the right shoulder.

Variation/progression
Practise lateral-angled zigzag runs.

DRILL   *KNEE-OUT SKIP*

Aim
To stretch the inner thigh and improve hip mobility; to develop an angled knee drive, balance, co-ordination and rhythm; to increase body temperature.

Area/equipment
An indoor or outdoor grid 18 metres in length. The width of the grid is variable depending on the size of the squad.

Description
Players cover the length of the grid in a skipping motion. The knee moves from the centre of the body to a position outside the body before returning to the central position. The player then returns to the start by repeating the drill backwards.

Key teaching points
- Feet start facing forwards and move outwards as the knee is raised
- Work off the balls of the feet
- The knee should be pushed, not rolled, out and back
- Maintain correct arm mechanics (see pages 45–47)
- The movement should be smooth, not jerky

What you might see	Solution
Landing on the heels	Focus on landing on the balls of the feet, with the trunk leaning forwards
Leaning too far back	Keep the head slightly dipped towards the chest

Sets and reps
2 x 18 metres: 1 forwards and 1 backwards.

Variation/progression
Perform the drill laterally.

DRILL   PRE-TURN

Aim
To prepare the hips for a turning action without committing the whole body; to increase body temperature; to improve body control.

Area/equipment
An indoor or outdoor grid 18 metres in length. The width of the grid is variable depending on the size of the squad.

Description
Players cover the length of the grid by performing a lateral movement. The heel of the back foot is moved to a position almost alongside the lead foot. Just before the feet come together, the lead foot is moved away sideways. Return to the start by repeating the drill, but lead with the opposite shoulder.

Key teaching points
- The back foot must not cross the lead foot
- Work off the balls of the feet
- Maintain correct arm mechanics
- Maintain an upright posture
- Do not sink into the hips or fold at the waist
- Do not use a high knee lift; the angle should be no more than 45 degrees

What you might see	Solution
Crossing of feet	Player to focus on a stepping rather than a skipping motion; use marker spots to indicate where feet should be placed in pre-turn stepping
Leading leg raised	Use the arm on the leading side to press down on the thigh as a reminder that this leg remains straighter
Hips turned	Stand tall with the head up, breathe in and out then hold the contraction

Sets and reps
2 x 18 metres: 1 leading with the left shoulder and 1 leading with the right shoulder.

DRILL RUSSIAN WALK

Aim
To stretch the back of the thighs; to improve hip mobility and stabilise the ankle; to develop balance and co-ordination; to increase body temperature.

Area/equipment
An indoor or outdoor grid 18 metres in length. The width of the grid is variable depending on the size of the squad.

Description
Players cover the length of the grid by performing a walking march with a high extended step. Imagine that the aim is to scrape the sole of your shoes down the front of a door or a fence.

Key teaching points
- Lift the knee before extending the leg
- Work off the balls of the feet
- Try to keep off the heels, particularly on the back foot
- Keep the hips square
- Pull the toes of the extended leg towards the shin so that they are vertical

What you might see
- Toes pointing out horizontally, not vertically

Solution
- Get the player to pull the toes towards the shin, and practise the Russian Walk on the spot before trying it on the move

Sets and reps
2 x 18 metres, both forwards.

Variation/progression
Perform the drill backwards.

DRILL   *WALKING LUNGE*

Aim
To stretch the front of the hips and thighs; to develop balance and co-ordination; to increase body temperature.

Area/equipment
An indoor or outdoor grid 18 metres in length. The width of the grid is variable depending on the size of the squad.

Description
Players cover the length of the grid by performing a walking lunge. The front leg should be bent with a 90-degree angle at the knee and the thigh in a horizontal position. The back leg should also be bent at a 90-degree angle, but with the knee touching the ground and the thigh in a vertical position. During the lunge the player brings both arms above the head to activate the core muscles. Return to the start by repeating the drill backwards.

Key teaching points
- Keep the hips square
- Maintain a strong core and keep upright
- Maintain good control
- Persevere with backward lunges – they are difficult to master
- Keep the trunk in an upright position

What you might see	Solution
Poor balance and control	Over-striding can cause this. Ensure that players bend the knee at a 90-degree angle and that the thigh is in the horizontal position. Use Marker Spots to indicate the length of the lunge
Stride too short, causing inability to lunge properly	Focus on a 90-degree knee bend and ensure that the thigh is horizontal. Practise the drill slowly on the spot if poor form continues

Sets and reps
2 x 18 metres: 1 forwards and 1 backwards.

Variations/progressions
- Perform the drill while holding hand weights
- Perform the drill while catching and passing a ball in the 'down' position
- Alternate arms above the head, one up and one down

DRILL   *SIDE LUNGE*

Aim
To stretch the inner thighs and gluteals (buttocks); to develop balance and co-ordination; to increase body temperature.

Area/equipment
An indoor or outdoor grid 18 metres in length. The width of the grid is variable depending on the size of the squad.

Description
Players cover the length of the grid by performing lateral lunges: take a wide lateral step and simultaneously lower the gluteals towards the ground. Return to the start leading with the opposite shoulder.

Key teaching points
- Do not bend at the waist or lean forwards
- Try to keep off the heels
- Maintain a strong core and keep upright
- Use the arms primarily for balance

What you might see   Solution
- Players leaning forwards
- Keep the spine in an upright, aligned position by keeping the head up and the chin level

Sets and reps
2 x 18 metres: 1 leading with the left shoulder and 1 leading with the right shoulder.

Variation/progression
Work in pairs facing each other and chest-passing a ball.

DRILL | HURDLE WALK

Aim

To stretch the inner and outer thighs and increase ROM; to develop balance and co-ordination; to increase body temperature.

Area/equipment

An indoor or outdoor grid 18 metres in length. The width of the grid is variable depending on the size of the squad.

Description

Players cover the length of the grid by walking in a straight line and lifting alternate legs as if going over high hurdles, then return to the start by repeating the drill backwards.

Key teaching points

- Try to keep the body square as the hips rotate
- Work off the balls of the feet
- Maintain an upright posture
- Do not sink into the hips or bend over at the waist
- Imagine that you are actually stepping over a barrier

What you might see

- Anchored foot is flat while the other leg is raised, causing a poor ROM

Solution

- Player should focus on working off the ball of the foot that is anchored. Practise this by getting the players to stand with their feet shoulder-width apart, rise up off their heels onto the balls of the feet, hold for a second and then return to the starting position; repeat 20–30 times. This will provide kinaesthetic feedback to the players about what it feels like to be on the balls of the feet

Sets and reps

2 x 18 metres: 1 forwards and 1 backwards.

DRILL   *WALKING HAMSTRING*

Aim
To stretch the backs of the thighs.

Area/equipment
An indoor or outdoor grid 18 metres in length. The width of the grid is variable depending on the size of the squad.

Description
Players cover the length of the grid by extending the lead leg heel-first onto the ground, rolling onto the ball of the foot and sinking into the hips, keeping the spine upright. Walk forwards and repeat on the opposite leg; continue in this manner, alternating the lead leg. For comfort, cross the arms.

Key teaching points
■ Keep the spine straight
■ Do not bend over
■ Control the head by looking forwards at all times
■ Work at a steady pace; do not rush

What you might see	Solution
■ Players with their head down, leaning forwards	■ Player should keep the chin up and focus on something horizontally in line with the eyes
■ Bending at the waist	■ Hips should be kept square; the trunk and spine must be kept upright

Sets and reps
2 x 18 metres: 1 forwards and 1 backwards.

Variation/progression
Perform the drill laterally.

DRILL HAMSTRING BUTTOCK FLICKS

Aim
To stretch the front and back of the thighs; to improve hip mobility; to increase body temperature.

Area/equipment
An indoor or outdoor grid 18 metres in length. The width of the grid is variable depending on the size of the squad.

Description
Players cover the length of the grid by moving forwards using alternating leg flicks, where the heel moves up towards the buttocks, then returns to the start by repeating the drill backwards.

Key teaching points
- Start slowly and gradually increase the tempo
- Work off the balls of the feet
- Maintain an upright posture
- Do not sink into the hips
- Try to develop a rhythm

What you might see	Solution
Knee raised up towards the front of the body	The thigh should remain vertical to the ground with the movement starting from below the knee. Practise the leg flick while standing still, using a wall or a partner for stability, and get the players to look down and observe the movement required
Hands held at the back above the top of the thighs	Use of the ball should help prevent this negative action; remind players that they do not move with their hands behind their back during a game

Sets and reps
2 x 18 metres: 1 forwards and 1 backwards.

Variations/Progressions
- Perform the drill laterally.
- Perform the drill as above, but flick the heel to the outside of the buttocks.

DRILL CARIOCA

Aim
To improve hip mobility and speed, which will increase the firing of nerve impulses over a period of time; to develop balance and co-ordination while moving and twisting; to increase body temperature.

Area/equipment
An indoor or outdoor grid 18 metres in length. The width of the grid is variable depending on the size of the squad.

Description
Players cover the length of the grid by moving laterally. The rear foot crosses in front of the body and then moves around to the back. Simultaneously, the lead foot does the opposite. The arms also move across the front and back of the body.

Key teaching points
- Start slowly and gradually increase the tempo
- Work off the balls of the feet
- Keep the shoulders square
- Do not force the ROM
- Use the arms primarily for balance

What you might see	Solution
Sinking into the hips	Stand tall with the head up, breathe in and out and hold the contraction
Co-ordination problems, e.g. inability to put second leg behind front leg	Practise slowly; go through the drill at walking pace
Arms swung too quickly or not at all	Allow the arms to do what comes naturally

Sets and reps
2 x 18 metres: 1 leading with the left leg and 1 leading with the right leg.

Variation/progression
Perform the drill laterally with a partner (mirror drills), i.e. one initiates/leads the movement while the other attempts to follow.

DRILL LEG OUT AND ACROSS THE BODY

Aim
To increase ROM in the hip region; to increase body temperature.

Area/equipment
A wall or fence to lean against.

Description
Players face and lean against a wall or fence at a 20–30-degree angle and swing one leg across the body from one side to the other. Repeat on the other leg. As seen in this photo, they may also use another player as support.

Key teaching points
■ Do not force an increased ROM
■ Work off the ball of the support foot
■ Lean with both hands against the wall/fence
■ Keep the hips square
■ Do not look down
■ Gradually increase the speed of the movement

What you might see	Solution
■ No heel raise off the ground	■ Get player to focus on leaning forwards and transferring their weight onto the ball of the foot while the other leg is swung across the body

Sets and reps
7–10 on each leg: work one leg and then the other.

Variation/progression
Lean against a partner, as shown in the photograph – but be careful how the leg is swung!

DRILL
WALL DRILLS –
LINEAR LEG FORWARDS AND BACK

Aim
To increase ROM in the hip region; to increase body temperature.

Area/equipment
A wall or fence to lean against.

Description
Players face and lean against the wall or fence at a 20–30-degree angle or use another player as support, take the leg back and swing it forwards in a linear motion along the same plane. Repeat with the other leg.

Key teaching points
- Do not force an increased ROM
- Work off the ball of the support foot
- Lean with both hands against the wall/fence
- Do not look down
- Gradually increase the speed of the movement

What you might see
- No heel raise off the ground

Solution
- Get player to focus on leaning forwards and transferring their weight onto the ball of the foot while the other leg is swung across the body

Sets and reps
7–10 on each leg: work one leg and then the other.

Variation/progression
Lean against a partner as shown in the photograph – but be careful how the leg is swung!

DRILL WALL DRILLS – KNEE ACROSS BODY

Aim
To increase ROM in the hip region; to increase body temperature.

Area/equipment
A wall or fence to lean against.

Description
Players face and lean against the wall or fence at a 20–30-degree angle or use another player for support and, from a standing position, drive one knee upwards and across the body. Repeat with the other leg.

Key teaching points
- Do not force an increased ROM
- Work off the ball of the support foot
- Lean with both hands against the wall/fence
- Keep the hips square
- Do not look down
- Gradually increase the speed of the movement
- Imagine you are trying to get your knee up and across the body to the opposite hip

What you might see	Solution
■ No heel raise off the ground	■ Get player to focus on leaning forwards and transferring their weight onto the ball of the foot while the other leg is swung across the body

Sets and reps
7–10 on each leg: work one leg and then the other.

Variation/progression
Lean against a partner as shown in the photograph – but be careful how the leg is swung!

DRILL PAIR DRILLS – LATERAL PAIR RUNS

Aim
To develop running skills in a more game-specific situation; to stimulate balance and co-ordination; to practise reassertion of the correct mechanics after an interruption; to increase body temperature.

Area/equipment
An indoor or outdoor grid 18 metres in length. The width of the grid is variable depending on the size of the squad.

Description
Players face each other approximately 1 metre apart and cover the length of the grid by taking short lateral steps. Occasionally, one player can push the other.

Key teaching points
■ Refer to lateral running drills (see pages 52–53)
■ When off-balance or after being pushed, the focus should be on the reassertion of the correct arm and foot mechanics (see pages 31–62)

Sets and reps
2 x 18 metres: 1 leading with the left leg and 1 leading with the right leg.

Variation/progression
Introduce the ball: the players pass it hand to hand and then hand to foot.

DRILL   PAIR DRILLS – JOCKEYING

Aim
To simulate defensive and attacking close-quarter movement patterns; to increase body temperature.

Area/equipment
An indoor or outdoor grid 18 metres in length. The width of the grid is variable depending on the size of the squad.

Description
Players stand facing each other and cover the grid, working both forwards and backwards. The player moving forwards (attacker) will show the left shoulder and then the right shoulder alternately in a rhythmic motion. The player moving backwards (defender) covers the attacking player by reversing the movements.

Key teaching points
- Take short steps
- Do not cross the feet
- Maintain a strong core and an upright posture
- Do not sink into the hips
- Keep the eyes on the opponent at all times

Sets and reps
2 x 18 metres: 1 leading with the left keg and 1 leading with the right leg.

Variation/progression
Introduce the ball to the attacking player, who presses with the ball at his/her feet, transferring it from left to right to keep the defender on his/her toes.

DRILL **SELECTION OF SPRINTS**

Aim
To increase the intensity of the warm-up and to prepare players for maximum exertion; to speed up the firing rate of neuromuscular messages; to increase body temperature.

Area/equipment
An indoor or outdoor grid 18 metres in length. The width of the grid is variable depending on the size of the squad.

Description
Players sprint one way only, then perform a jog-back recovery back down the grid. Players should start from different angles, e.g. side-on, backwards etc., and accelerate into a forward running motion down the grid.

Key teaching points
■ Maintain good running mechanics (see pages 48–62)
■ Ensure that players alternate the lead foot

Sets and reps
1 set of 5 sprints, varying the start position.

Variations/progressions
■ Include swerving sprints
■ Include turns in the sprints
■ Include pressing sprints. Place 3 or 4 mannequins in a straight line 2 yards apart. Players form 3–4 single-file lines facing the mannequins, about 14 metres away from them. On the coach's call, the first line of players accelerate together and press the corresponding mannequins. The next line then repeats the drill. Each player should perform 4–5 presses in total.

CHAPTER 2 MECHANICS OF MOVEMENT

THE DEVELOPMENT OF RUNNING FORM FOR FOOTBALL

Do not take it for granted that players have been taught how to run correctly or that it is something that occurs naturally. You will always encounter natural, 'genetically gifted' players who are explosive and who make running quickly look easy, but these are few and far between. To neglect running mechanics in your football training is to ignore the potential in many of your players. How often do you hear comments such as 'good player but slow', 'he/she falls back on their heels' or 'not quick enough over the first few metres'. All players, whatever their age, can improve their speed and acceleration by using and practising the correct running mechanics.

The best players and teams in the world are able to vary the pace of their play effectively. They inject explosive phases and controlled deceleration; this allows them constantly to vary the speed of the game to suit the situation. The most successful teams, and the ones most difficult to beat, are those that can play at a high intensity while attacking, defending, tackling and supporting the ball. These are the teams that are in your face, in your space, throughout the game. Indeed, the demands of the game are continually changing: recent statistics provide the following information on movement in a game of football:

MOVEMENT STATISTICS IN A GAME OF FOOTBALL

Movement	Percentage of the game	Average speed
Walking/standing	28	4 km/h
Jogging	26	8 km/h
Running: low speed	21	12 km/h
Running: moderate speed	14	16 km/h
Running: high speed	6	21 km/h
Running: sprint	3	30 km/h
Running: backwards	2	–

Footballers do not continuously run at the same pace. Football is an intermittent, multi-movement game in which players are expected not only to run at different intensities, but also to tackle, pass, dribble, head and shoot. In a game, they perform more than 1,000 changes in activity and use over 420 different patterns of movement. The ball is in play for less than 60 minutes, with average bursts of activity lasting between four and six seconds over distances of 14–18 metres. On average, a player will touch the ball for less than two minutes per game. A forward will sprint more than a midfielder, who will, however, cover a greater distance. All of these statistics highlight the importance of correct mechanics in running, which in turn impacts on an individual's economy of movement and effectiveness in covering the ground.

There is no need to focus on the techniques required for a 90-metre sprint. Players very rarely have the space to plane out (achieve maximum maintainable speed) after 25 metres or relax and think about 'jelly jaw' techniques; instead, football requires a sound basic technique, together with the ability to change from correct running mechanics to holding off a player, using the arms for balance with the ball at the feet, and then reasserting good mechanics to re-accelerate.

The player who can explode over the first few metres will always be the one in front. I will never forget an interview with Mickey Quinn, then of Coventry City, who was famous for his large frame and ample stomach but who was top scorer in the Premiership. When asked how he did it, his reply was that he was the quickest over the first 5 metres. The first 5 metres are crucial because this is when a great deal of energy, force and power are used to propel the body forwards. During this initial phase (the acceleration phase), emphasis should be placed on a short stride length and a high stride frequency. As the player accelerates, stride length will increase

and strike frequency will decrease, resulting in the player covering a greater distance with each stride until they achieve maximum speed. Correct stride length and frequency are vital for effective and efficient running.

Mechanics for football

ARM MECHANICS

Good running form for football is not all about leg work. Power and balance come from the upper body, so encourage the following techniques in your players:

- elbows should be bent at a 90-degree angle

- hands and shoulders should be relaxed

- the inside of the wrist should brush against the hips

- the hands should move from the buttock cheeks to the chest or head

LIFT MECHANICS

Football is a multi-sprint, stop-and-start sport, so the first phase of acceleration and re-acceleration is crucial. Coaching players to get their knees up high, particularly in the first few yards of the acceleration phase, only makes them slower. It has the negative effect of minimising force development, so that insufficient power is produced to propel the body forwards in an explosive action. During the first few metres of acceleration, short, sharp steps are required. These generate a high degree of force, which takes the body from a stationery position into the first controlled explosive steps. Look and listen for the following in a player's initial acceleration strides:

- 45-degree knee lift

- knees coming up in a vertical line

- front of the foot staying in a linear (forward-facing) position

- on the lift, the foot will transfer from pointing slightly down to pointing slightly up

- if the foot or the knee splays in or out, this means that power will not be transferred correctly

- foot-to-floor contacts with the ball of the foot

- keep off the heels

- foot-to-floor contact makes a tapping noise, not a thud or a slap

POSTURE

Posture is another important element of acceleration and sprinting. The spine should be kept as straight as possible at all times. This means that a player who has tackled, jockeyed or jumped for the ball and now wants to run into space needs to transfer to correct running form as quickly as possible. Running with a straight spine does not mean running bolt upright; you can keep your spine straight using a slight lean forwards. What *is* to be avoided is players 'sinking into their hips', which looks like running 'folded up at the middle', because this prevents effective transfer of power.

MECHANICS FOR DECELERATION

The ability of a footballer to stop quickly, change direction and accelerate away from an opponent is key. You can practise this: do not leave it to chance, include it in your sessions.

Posture

Lean back. This alters the angle of the spine and hips, which control foot placement. Foot contact with the ground will now transfer to the heel, which acts like a brake.

Fire the arms

By firing the arms quickly, the energy produced will increase the frequency of heel contacts to the ground. Think of it like pressing harder on the brakes in a car.

MECHANICS FOR JUMPING

As with running, arm drive is crucial for an efficient jumping technique. Both arms should move together through an arc from the hips to the ears in an explosive, upward, driving motion. This technique raises the body's centre of gravity, transferring a downward force through the hips and legs into an upward force that enables maximal upward thrust. The trick is to maintain an upright position, use only a slight bend at the knees and simultaneously power off the balls of the feet. It is important to remember not to sink too deeply into the hips on landing, as this will prevent a quick repeat jump or acceleration away from the landing.

LATERAL SIDE-STEP

Do not use a wide stance as this will decrease the potential for power generation as you attempt to push off/away. Do not pull with the leading foot, but rather push off the back foot. Imagine that your car has broken down and that you need to move it to a service station – would you pull it? No, you would push it. Ensure that a strong arm drive is used at all times, but particularly during the push-off phase.

MAKING A 180-DEGREE TURN – THE DROP STEP

Most players use too many movements to make 180-degree turns. Many jump up on the spot first, then take three or four steps to make the turn; others will jump up and perform the turn in the air with a complete lack of control. When practised, the drop step turn looks seamless and is far quicker.

For a right shoulder turn, the player starts by

opening up the right groin and simultaneously transferring the weight onto the left foot. The right foot is raised slightly off the ground and, using a swinging action, is moved around to the right to face the opposite direction. The right foot is planted and the player drives/pushes off the left foot, remembering to use a strong arm drive. Do not overstretch on the turn. Players may find it helpful initially to tell themselves to 'turn and go'. With practice, players will develop an efficient and economic seamless turn.

Fundamental movement checklists for players

These movement checklists for players will help coaches and trainers identify the correct and incorrect form for multi-directional movement. They also provide solutions that can be implemented easily to rectify the problems. These solutions can be used with players of all ages and abilities. If you are ever in doubt regarding a player's movement, you must consult a physiotherapist or doctor to ensure that there are no physiological problems that may require medical intervention. Where you see odd movement patterns, it is important to try to assess how long it takes the individual to re-assert positive movement patterns. The longer it takes, the more likely the movement of the player will seem slower and less effective.

The movement checklists can be used in all areas of the SAQ Continuum, including explosion when resistance equipment is being used. The golden rule is that correct mechanics and form always come first.

RUNNING – STARTING POSITION

Correct	Incorrect	Solution
FEET POSITION ■ Shoulder-width apart	■ Too wide ■ Too close	■ Use chalk marks or Marker Spots on the surface to indicate best position
■ On the ball of the foot	■ On the toes ■ On the heels ■ Weight outside or inside	■ Lean slightly forwards on the balls of the feet ■ Position feet in a straight, linear position ■ Lean slightly forwards on the balls of the feet. Heels off the ground
■ Straight, linear	■ Pointing in ■ Splayed out	■ Use straight lines to position feet so they point in a straight, linear direction ■ Use chalk to mark around the foot on hard surfaces so the outline can be stood in to ensure correct positioning
ARMS ■ Held ready, 90° at the elbow ■ One forwards, one back ■ Relaxed	■ Arms by the side ■ Shoulders shrugged with arms too high ■ Tight and restricted	■ Provide constant feedback on arm technique ■ Practise holding arms in correct position, then accelerate arms as if starting to run (see Partner arm-drive drill, page 45) ■ Use string looped around index finger and thumb and point of elbow to hold correct position of 90°
HIPS ■ Need to be high or tall and slightly forwards	■ Sunk ■ Twisted	■ Hold head tall and upright ■ Stomach held in; focus on keeping the hips held high and leaning slightly forwards in the direction of running. ■ Keep the chin off the chest ■ Focus on good linear body position
HEAD POSITION ■ Held high ■ Eyes forwards	■ Held down, turned ■ Looking up	■ Imagine you are looking over a fence that comes up to your nose ■ Pick an object in the distance and focus on it

RUNNING – ACCELERATION PHASE

Correct	Incorrect	Solution
HANDS ■ Fingertips gently touching thumb tip	■ Soft (most common) ■ Droopy ■ DroopyTightly closed	■ Hold post-it note or something similar between index finger and thumb
ARM ACTION ■ Fast ■ 90° angle at elbow ■ Hand above shoulder ■ One forwards, one back behind hips	■ Slow to medium	■ Use Partner arm-drive drills (see page 45) ■ Use short, sharp sets of fast on-the-spot arm bursts ■ Use light hand weights for 8–9 seconds, then perform contrast arm drives as quickly as possible afterwards
ARM DRIVE ■ Chin to waist ■ Wrist or hand firm	■ Arms across body ■ Forearm chop ■ At the side ■ Held in stiff angled position	■ Perform Partner arm-drive drills (see page 45) ■ Brush the inside of the wrist against the waist band, then touch thumb to chin ■ Loop large elastic bands from between index and thumb to elbow, then perform arm drives ■ Perform arm drive drills in front of a mirror for feedback ■ Perform Buttock bounces (see page 47)
HEAD ■ Held high ■ Kept up ■ Eyes forwards	■ Held down ■ Turned ■ Looking up ■ Rocking from side to side	■ Imagine you are looking over a fence that comes up to your nose ■ Pick an object in the distance and focus on it
BODY POSITION ■ Tall ■ Strong	■ Sunk ■ Soft ■ Bent	■ Keep the head up ■ Hold the stomach in ■ Keep the hips high, slightly forwards and square
FOOT ACTION ■ Active – plantar flex (toe down); dorsi flex (toe up)	■ Flat ■ Heel first to touch ground ■ Inactive plantar/dorsi flex	■ Focus on the balls of the feet ■ Remove built-up heeled shoes ■ Practise plantar/dorsi flex skip ■ Ensure there is a slight forward body lean ■ Keep the head up; do not sink into the hips

Contd...

Contd...

Correct	Incorrect	Solution
HEELS ■ Raised	■ Down, contacting ground first	■ Focus on the balls of the feet ■ Remove built-up heeled shoes ■ Roll up cloth or paper and use tape to form it into a small ball, slightly larger than a marble. Place in shoes under the heels
HIPS ■ Tall ■ Square ■ Up/forwards ■ Firm ■ Still	■ Bent ■ Sunk ■ Turned	■ Hold head tall and upright ■ Hold stomach in and focus on keeping the hips held square to the running direction ■ Practise Buttock bounces (see page 47)
KNEES ■ Linear ■ Below waist ■ Foot just off ground ■ Drive forwards	■ Across body ■ Splayed ■ Too high with foot too high off ground	■ Practise Dead-leg run (see page 48) ■ Teacher/coach to place hands above where knees should go; practise bringing the knees up to the hands by running on the spot ■ Stick coloured tape from above the knee to below the knee in a straight line, on either the skin or clothing. The tape should go across the centre of the kneecap. Now perform on-the-spot running drills in front of a mirror, focusing on keeping the coloured tape in a straight line
RELAXATION ■ Relaxed ■ Calm ■ Comfortable	■ Tense ■ Too loose ■ Distracted	■ Imagine accelerating quickly with power and grace, but calm and relaxed ■ Breathing controlled

AFTER ACCELERATION: PLANING OUT PHASE

Correct	Incorrect	Solution
STRIDE LENGTH ■ Medium for individual	■ Too long ■ Too short ■ Erratic	■ Use Marker Spots or Stride Frequency Canes to mark out correct stride length
STRIDE FREQUENCY ■ Balanced for individual	■ Too quick ■ Too slow	■ Use Marker Spots or Stride Frequency Canes to mark out correct stride length so that frequency can be determined
ARM ACTION ■ Fast ■ 90° angle at elbow ■ Hand goes from above shoulder to behind hips	■ Slow to medium	■ Perform Partner arm-drive drills (see page 45) ■ Use short, sharp sets of on-the-spot fast arm bursts ■ Use light hand weights for 8–9 seconds, then perform contrast arm drives as soon as possible afterwards
ARM DRIVE ■ Chin to waist	■ Arms across body ■ Forearm chop ■ At the side ■ Held in stiff angled position	■ Perform Partner arm drive drills (see page 45) ■ Brush the inside of the wrist against the waist band, then touch thumb to chin ■ Loop large elastic bands from between index finger and thumb and elbow, then perform arm drives ■ Perform arm drive drills in front of a mirror for feedback ■ Perform Buttock bounces (see page 47)
HEAD ■ Held high, kept up ■ Eyes forwards	■ Held down ■ Turned ■ Looking up ■ Rocking from side to side	■ Imagine you are looking over a fence that comes up to your nose ■ Pick an object in the distance and focus on it
BODY POSITION – TRUNK ■ Tall	■ Sunk ■ Soft ■ Bent	■ Keep the head up ■ Hold the stomach in ■ Keep the hips high, slightly forwards and square

Contd...

Contd...

Correct	Incorrect	Solution
FOOT ACTION ■ Active – plantar flex (toe down) and dorsi-flex (toe up)	■ Flat ■ Heel first to touch ground ■ Inactive plantar/dorsi flex	■ Focus on the balls of the feet ■ Remove built-up heeled shoes ■ Practise plantar/dorsi flex skip ■ Ensure there is a slight forward body lean ■ Keep the head up; do not sink into the hips
RELAXATION ■ Relaxed ■ Calm ■ Comfortable	■ Tense ■ Too loose ■ Distracted	■ Imagine accelerating quickly with power and grace, but calm and relaxed ■ Keep breathing controlled

LATERAL STEPPING

Correct	Incorrect	Solution
FOOT ACTION ■ Work off the balls of the feet	■ On the heels ■ Flat footed	■ Lean slightly forwards even when stepping sideways ■ Provide constant feedback to keep off the heels ■ Keep the hips tall and strong; this helps to control power and prevent flat-footed weight transfer
■ Feet shoulder-width apart	■ Too wide ■ Too close ■ Crossed ■ Pointing in ■ Splayed out	■ Use Marker Spots to indicate best foot position ■ Practise stepping slowly at first and build up speed gradually
■ Drive off trailing foot	■ Reach with leading foot ■ Flat footed ■ On heels ■ Feet pointing in or splayed	■ Use Marker Spots to indicate best foot position ■ Stick coloured tape in a straight line from the tongue of the shoes to the end of the shoes. Work in front of mirror, focusing on keeping the lines on the foot straight ■ Place a taped ball of paper under the heel of each foot ■ Use angled boards to step off

Contd...

Contd...

Correct	Incorrect	Solution
HIPS ■ Firm ■ Controlled ■ Square ■ High	■ Soft ■ Twisted ■ Angled ■ Leaning too far forwards ■ Bent at the waist ■ Sunk	■ Hold head tall ■ Hold stomach in ■ Focus on keeping the hips square
ARMS ■ 90° arm drive (same as for lateral stepping) ■ Fast and strong drive	■ Arm across the body ■ No arm drive at all ■ Arms too tight and restricted ■ Arms moving forwards but not driving backwards behind the hips	■ Perform Partner arm drive drills (see page 45), practising moving sideways ■ Perform Mirror drills (see page 46) ■ Provide constant positive feedback
TRUNK ■ Strong and firm ■ Slight forward lean	■ Too upright ■ Leaning too far forward ■ Bent at the waist ■ Leaning back	■ Perform Mirror drills (see page 46) ■ Keep the head still and looking forwards ■ Hold the stomach in ■ Slight knee bend only

LATERAL TURNING – 90 DEGREES

Correct	Incorrect	Solution
FEET ■ Shoulder-width apart	■ Together ■ Too wide ■ Crossed	■ Use chalk marks or Marker Spots to indicate best starting and finishing position
ON THE TURN ■ Feet stay shoulder-width apart ■ Work on balls of feet	■ Come together ■ Cross ■ Go apart too wide ■ Go onto heels ■ Go onto toes	■ Use chalk marks or Marker Spots to indicate best starting and finishing position ■ Practise single turn in front of a mirror
FOOT DRIVE ■ Drive off trailing foot	■ Forward reach ■ Jump on the spot ■ Rock back on the heels	■ Keep the trunk firm ■ Get individuals to say the words 'push' on the drive and 'off' on the turn. This can be said in the head or out loud ■ Practise lateral side-steps slowly and gradually build up speed ■ Maintain a good arm drive
HIPS ■ High, slightly forwards and square ■ Hip before knee	■ Hips low and sunk ■ Angled, not square ■ Trunk leaning too far forwards or too upright	■ Keep the hips firm, tall and leaning forwards ■ Use arm drive with hips to assist turn ■ Keep hips square when turning ■ Practise turns slowly at first
HEAD ■ Kept up ■ Off the chest ■ Eyes looking forwards ■ Head and hip work simultaneously during turn	■ Floppy ■ Down ■ Angled ■ Back	■ Pick two distant objects, one in front of you, the other in the direction you are turning to. Initially, focus on the object in front; on the turn, refocus onto the second object

180-DEGREE TURN

Correct	Incorrect	Solution
INITIAL MOVEMENT ■ Seamless ■ Smooth ■ Sequence is drop, step and go (1–2–3)	■ Jump up ■ Step back ■ Twist	■ Practise drop step: the opening of the leg to point in the direction of the turn. The trailing foot then pushes off ■ Practise saying out loud 'drop, step and go' ■ Practise slowly at first, gradually developing speed ■ Practise facing a wall, so when you turn the back step is prevented ■ Practise the turn in front of a mirror ■ Use a video of the turn
FEET ■ Shoulder-width apart	■ Together ■ Too wide ■ Crossed	■ Use chalk marks or Marker Spots to indicate best starting and finishing position
ARM DRIVE ■ 90° arm drive, same as lateral stepping ■ Fast and strong drive	■ Arm across the body ■ No arm drive at all ■ Arms too tight and restricted ■ Arms moving forwards but not driving backwards behind the hips	■ Perform Partner arm drive drills (see page 45), practising moving sideways ■ Perform Mirror drills (see page 46) ■ Provide constant positive feedback
HEAD ■ Up ■ Eyes looking forwards	■ Down ■ Angled ■ Turned	■ Pick two distant objects, one in front of you, the other behind. Initially, focus on the object in front; on the turn, refocus onto the second object (behind)
HIPS ■ High, slightly forwards and square ■ Hip before knee	■ Hip low and sunk ■ Angled, not square ■ Trunk leaning too far forwards or too upright	■ Keep hips firm, tall and leaning forwards ■ Use arm drive with hips to assist turn ■ Keep hips square when turning ■ Practise turns slowly at first

JUMPING

Correct	Incorrect	Solution
ARM DRIVE ■ Arms at 90°, working together from behind the hips to above the head	■ No arm movement ■ Arms not working together ■ Only one arm used	■ Practise with a balloon. Hold the balloon in front of you, below the chest, with both hands, and then throw the balloon over the back of the head ■ Once the balloon drill is perfected, introduce throwing the balloon with a jump ■ Show the differences of jumping with arm drive and then without arm drive. Attempt a jump with arms at the side, then repeat with positive arm action
PRE-JUMP HIPS ■ Tall, slightly forwards	■ Bent ■ Sunk (most common)	■ Keep hips firm, tall and leaning forwards ■ Keep hips square when jumping ■ Keep head up and hold stomach in
TAKE-OFF FEET ■ Ball of the foot	■ Flat footed ■ On the heels ■ On the toes	■ Provide constant feedback to keep off heels ■ Keep the hips tall and strong; this helps control power and prevent flat-footed weight transfer ■ Use a small round stick or old books 1.5 cm thick. Place under both heels so that weight is forced onto the ball of the foot. Practise jumping in this position
LANDING ■ Balls of the feet ■ Weight equally balanced on both feet when possible	■ On the toes ■ Heels ■ Unbalanced	■ Practise multiple bunny hops, landing on the balls of the feet, for correct foot-to-ground contact ■ Place a taped ball of paper (the size of a marble) under the heel of each foot ■ Draw small circles or use small Marker Spots 5–8 cm in diameter; use these as landing markers for the balls of the feet
TRUNK ■ Tall, hips leaning slightly forwards ■ Firm and relaxed	■ Sunk ■ Bent at the waist ■ Twisted ■ Uncontrolled	■ Breathe in and hold the stomach firm ■ Keep the head high

Contd...

Contd...

Correct	Incorrect	Solution
HIPS ■ Firm ■ Tall ■ Leaning slightly forwards	■ Hips low and sunk ■ Angled, not square ■ Trunk leaning too far forwards or too upright	■ Keep hips firm, tall and leaning forwards ■ Use arm drive with hips to assist control ■ Keep hips square when landing ■ Practise landing by jumping off a step or small box ■ Visualise perfect body position

DECELERATION

Correct	Incorrect	Solution
ARMS ■ 90° angle ■ Increase speed of drive on deceleration	■ Slow arm drive ■ No arm drive ■ Arms dropped by the sides	■ Provide feedback of 'drive arms' as soon as deceleration commences ■ Use string or elastic bands looped around index and thumb and point of elbow to hold correct position of 90° ■ Use light hand weights that are released on the deceleration phase
FEET ■ Shorten stride to smaller steps	■ Maintain long strides	■ Use coloured canes or Marker Spots or a short piece of outdoor fast foot ladder on the deceleration phase
HEAD ■ Slightly raised above horizontal plane ■ Eyes up	■ Chin down on chest ■ Head turned to one side	■ Prior to deceleration phase, pick an object in the distance that is slightly higher than the horizon, therefore requiring the head to be brought up ■ Coach to call 'head up' as deceleration phase begins
HIPS ■ Lean back	■ Remaining forwards ■ Lop-sided ■ Sunk	■ Focus on bringing the head up; this will change the angle of the hips

Contd...

TRUNK		
■ Brought upright	■ Remaining tilted forwards ■ Bent	■ Focus on head up, trunk up and hips back. Work on this combination during deceleration
HEELS ■ Weight transferred to heel ■ Heel first to hit the ground	■ On the toes ■ Too much weight forwards on the balls of the feet	■ Get athlete to focus on head up, trunk up and hips back. Work on this combination during deceleration. This will also impact on the spine and transfer to the heel coming down to the ground first for deceleration

DRILL ARM MECHANICS – PARTNER DRILLS

Aim
To perfect the correct arm technique for running in football.

Area/equipment
The player works with a partner.

Description
Player stands with his partner behind him. The partner holds the palms of his hands in line with the player's elbows, fingers pointing upwards. The player fires the arms as if sprinting, so that the elbows 'smack' into the partner's palms.

Key teaching points
- The arms should not move across the body
- The elbows should be at a 90-degree angle
- The hands and shoulders should be relaxed
- The insides of the wrists should brush against the hips
- Ensure that the player performs a full ROM – the hands should move from the buttock cheeks to the chest or head
- Encourage speed of movement to hear the 'smack'

Sets and reps
3 sets of 16 reps with a 1-minute recovery between each set.

Variation/progression
Use light hand weights for the first two sets, then perform the last set without.

DRILL ARM MECHANICS – MIRROR DRILLS

Aim
To perfect the correct arm technique for running in football.

Area/equipment
A large mirror.

Description
Player stands in front of the mirror with his arms 'ready' for sprinting and performs short bursts of arm drives. Use the mirror as a feedback tool to perfect the technique.

Key teaching points
- The arms should not move across the body
- The elbows should be at a 90-degree angle
- The hands and shoulders should be relaxed
- The insides of the wrists should brush against the hips
- Ensure that the player performs a full ROM – the hands should move from the buttock cheeks to the chest or head

Sets and reps
3 sets of 16 reps with a 1-minute recovery between each set.

Variation/progression
Use light hand weights for the first two sets, then perform the last set without.

DRILL   ARM MECHANICS – BUTTOCK BOUNCES

Aim
To develop explosive arm drive.

Area/equipment
A suitable ground surface.

Description
Player sits on the floor with his legs straight out in front and fires the arms rapidly in short bursts. The power generated should be great enough to raise the buttocks off the floor in a bouncing manner.

Key teaching points
- The arms should not move across the body
- The elbows should be at a 90-degree angle
- The hands and shoulders should be relaxed
- The insides of the wrists should brush against the hips
- Ensure that the player performs a full ROM – the hands should move from the buttock cheeks to the chest or head
- Encourage speed of movement to hear the 'smack'

Sets and reps
3 sets of 6 reps – each rep is 6–8 explosive arm drives – with a 1-minute recovery between each set.

Variation/progression
Use light hand weights for the first 2 sets, then perform the last set without.

DRILL   *RUNNING FORM – SINGLE DEAD-LEG RUN*

Aim
To develop a quick knee lift and the positive foot placement required for effective sprinting.

Area/equipment
Indoor or outdoor area. Place approximately 8 V Hurdles at 0.5-metre intervals in a straight line. Place a marker 1 metre from each end of the line to mark the start and finish.

Description
Player must keep the outside leg straight in a 'locked' position. The inside leg moves over the obstacles in a cycling motion while the outside leg swings along just above the ground. See figure 2.1.

Key teaching points
- Bring the knee of the inside leg up to just below 90 degrees
- Point the toes upwards
- Bring the inside leg back down quickly between the V Hurdles
- Increase the speed of the movement once the technique has been mastered
- Maintain correct arm mechanics (see pages 45–47)
- Maintain an upright posture and a strong core
- Keep the hips square and stand tall

Sets and reps
1 set of 6 reps, 3 leading off the left leg and 3 leading off the right leg.

Variations/progressions
- Use light hand weights – accelerate off the end of the last V Hurdle and drop the hand weights during this acceleration phase
- Place several different-coloured markers 2 metres from the last V Hurdle at different angles. As the player leaves the last hurdle, the coach nominates a marker for the player to accelerate on to

Figure 2.1 Single dead-leg run

DRILL   *RUNNING FORM – PRE-TURN*

Aim

To educate and prepare the hips, legs and feet for effective and quick turning without fully committing the whole body; to maintain dynamic balance, keeping the centre of gravity over the base of support while the body is moving.

Area/equipment

Indoor or outdoor area. Place 8 V Hurdles at 0.5-metre intervals in a straight line. Place a marker 1 metre from each end of the line to mark the start and finish. See figure 2.2.

Description

Player moves sideways along the line of hurdles, just in front of them (i.e. not travelling over them). The back leg (following leg) is brought over the hurdle to a position slightly in front of the body so that the heel is in line with the toe of the leading foot. As the back foot is planted, the leading foot moves away. Repeat the drill with the opposite leg leading.

Key teaching points

- Stand tall and do not sink into the hips
- Do not allow the feet to cross over
- Keep the feet shoulder-width apart as much as possible
- The knee lift should be no greater than 45 degrees
- Maintain correct arm mechanics (see pages 45–47)
- Maintain an upright posture
- Keep the hips and shoulders square
- Work both the left and right sides

Sets and reps

1 set of 6 reps, 3 leading with the left shoulder and 3 leading with the right shoulder.

Variations/progressions

- Use light hand weights – at the end of the hurdles, turn and accelerate 5 metres. Drop the weights halfway through the acceleration phase
- Place several different-coloured markers 2 metres from the last hurdle at different angles. As the player leaves the last hurdle, the coach nominates a marker for the player to accelerate on to
- Work in pairs. Partner stands 2 metres from the first hurdle with a ball held out in each hand above the shoulders. As the player leaves the last hurdle, the partner drops one of the balls. The player accelerates to trap the ball

Figure 2.2 Pre-turn

DRILL | *RUNNING FORM – LEADING LEG RUN*

Aim
To develop quick, efficient steps and running techniques.

Area/equipment
Indoor or outdoor area. Place approximately 8 V Hurdles at 0.5-metre intervals in a straight line. Place a marker 1 metre from each end of the line to mark the start and finish.

Description
Player runs down the line of hurdles, crossing over each one with the same lead leg. The aim is to just clear the hurdles. Repeat the drill using the opposite leg as the lead. See figure 2.3.

Key teaching points
■ The knee lift should be to no more than 45 degrees
■ Use short, sharp steps
■ Maintain strong arm mechanics (see pages 45–47)
■ Maintain an upright posture
■ Stand tall and do not sink into the hips

Sets and reps
1 set of 6 reps, 3 leading with the left leg and 3 leading with the right leg.

Variations/progressions
■ To practise changing direction after running in a straight line, place 3 markers 2–3 metres away from the end of the hurdles at different angles; on leaving the last hurdle, the player sprints out to the marker nominated by the coach
■ Vary the distance between the hurdles to achieve different stride lengths

Figure 2.3 Leading leg run

DRILL *RUNNING FORM –*
QUICK SIDE-STEP DEVELOPMENT

Aim
To develop correct, precise and controlled lateral steps; to maintain dynamic balance, keeping the centre of gravity over the base of support while the body is moving; to allow a player to recover from one lateral movement into a movement in the other direction.

Area/equipment
Indoor or outdoor area. Place 3 V Hurdles side by side, about 1 metre apart.

Description
Player stands on the outside of hurdle 1, so that he will step over the middle of each hurdle. The player performs lateral movement mechanics while clearing each hurdle. On clearing the third hurdle, he repeats the drill in the opposite direction.

Key teaching points
■ Maintain correct lateral running form/mechanics (see pages 51–53)
■ Maintain correct arm mechanics (see pages 45–47)
■ Do not sink into the hips
■ Keep the head up
■ Do not lean too far forwards
■ Use small steps and work off the balls of the feet
■ Do not use an excessively high knee lift

Sets and reps
2 sets of 10 reps, 5 to the left and 5 to the right, with a 60-second recovery between sets.

Variations/progressions
■ Work with a coach or a team-mate who randomly directs the player over the hurdles
■ Work with a coach or a team-mate who randomly directs the player over the hurdles while passing a ball for the player to return
■ Add 2 more hurdles to add lift variations
■ Work in groups of 3 players: player 1 works through the hurdles, while players 2 and 3 stand at either end and pass a ball for player 1 to pass back as he gets to the end
■ Work in groups of 3 players: players 2 and 3 stand at opposite ends and opposite sides of the hurdles. Player 1 works through the hurdles, receiving the ball from and returning it to player 2. On stepping over the last hurdle, player 1 turns and receives the ball from player 3, returns it and then works back down the hurdles facing in the other direction. At the other end he repeats the turn and continues the drill

DRILL | *RUNNING FORM –* LATERAL SIDE-STEP DEVELOPMENT

Aim
To develop efficient and economical lateral side-steps when receiving and returning a ball.

Area/equipment
Indoor or outdoor area; balls. Place 8 Micro V Hurdles at 0.5-metre intervals in a straight line. Place a marker 1 metre from each end of the line to mark the start and finish.

Description
Player steps over each hurdle, moving sideways. See figure 2.4.

Key teaching points
■ Bring the knee up to just below 45 degrees
■ Do not skip sideways – step!
■ Push off from the back foot; do not pull with the lead foot
■ Maintain an upright posture
■ Keep the hips square
■ Do not sink into the hips

Sets and reps
1 set of 6 reps, 3 leading with the left shoulder and 3 leading with the right.

Variations/progressions
■ Use light hand weights and, after the last hurdle, perform a pivot step, drop the hand weights and accelerate off in the direction in which you are facing
■ Place several different-coloured markers 2 metres from the last hurdle. As the player leaves the last hurdle, the coach nominates a marker for the player to accelerate to and return a ball passed to them by the coach

Figure 2.4 Lateral side-step development

DRILL

RUNNING FORM –
LATERAL ANGLED STEP DEVELOPMENT

Aim
To develop efficient and economical lateral side-steps when receiving and returning a ball.

Area/equipment
Indoor or outdoor area; balls. Place 8 Micro V Hurdles side-on, 1 metre apart and staggered laterally. Position a finish Marker Spot or cone in the same pattern as the hurdles.

Description
Work in groups of 3. Player 1 works inside the channel created by the hurdles, stepping over each hurdle with one foot as he moves laterally down and across the channel. On stepping over the outside hurdle, a ball is passed to him, to be returned to player 2 who is situated on that side of the hurdles. This action is then repeated on the opposite side with player 3. After receiving the ball, players 2 and 3 walk backwards into position, ready for the next time player 1 steps over the outside hurdle. See figure 2.5.

Key teaching points
- Bring the knee up to a 45-degree angle over the hurdle
- Do not over-stride across the hurdles
- Maintain correct arm mechanics and a strong arm drive (see pages 45–47)
- Keep the hips square
- Do not sink into the hips

Sets and reps
2 sets of 6 reps with a walk-back recovery between reps and a 2-minute recovery between sets.

Variation/progression
Perform the drill backwards.

Figure 2.5 Lateral angled step development

DRILL RUNNING FORM – 1–2–3–LIFT

Aim
To develop an efficient leg cycle, rhythm, power, foot placement and dynamic balance.

Area/equipment
Indoor or outdoor area 15–20 metres in length.

Description
Player moves in a straight line; after every third step, the leg is brought up in an explosive action so that the knee is at a 90-degree angle. Continue the drill along the length prescribed, working the same leg, then repeat the drill leading with the other leg. See figure 2.6.

Key teaching points
- Keep the hips square
- Work off the balls of the feet
- Try to develop and maintain a rhythm
- Keep the eyes and head up and look ahead
- Maintain correct arm mechanics (see pages 45–47)
- Maintain an upright posture
- Leg to be snapped quickly up and down

Sets and reps
1 set of 6 reps, 3 leading with the left leg and 3 leading with the right leg.

Variations/progressions
- Alternate the lead leg during a repetition
- Vary the lift sequence, e.g. 1–2–3–4–lift, etc.

Figure 2.6 1–2–3–lift

DRILL   *JUMPING – SINGLE JUMPS*

Aim
To develop jumping techniques, power, speed, control and dynamic balance.

Area/equipment
Indoor or outdoor area. Ensure that the surface is clear of any obstacles. Use a 18- or 30-cm V Hurdle.

Description
Player jumps over a single hurdle and, on landing, walks back to the start point to repeat the drill. See figure 2.7(a).

Key teaching points
- Maintain good arm mechanics (see pages 45–47)
- Do not sink in to the hips at the take-off and landing phases
- Land on the balls of the feet
- Do not fall back onto the heels

Sets and reps
2 sets of 8 reps, with a 1-minute recovery between each set.

Variations/progressions
- Perform single jumps over the hurdle and back
- Perform single jumps over the hurdle with a 180-degree twist; practise twisting to both sides. See figure 2.7(b)
- Perform lateral single jumps – jump from both sides. See figure 2.7(c)

Figure 2.7(b) Single jumps with a 180-degree twist

Figure 2.7(a) Single jumps

Figure 2.7(c) Lateral single jumps

DRILL JUMPING – MULTIPLE HOPS AND JUMPS

Aim
To develop maximum control while taking off and landing; to develop controlled directional power and dynamic balance.

Area/equipment
Indoor or outdoor area. Place six to eight 18- or 30-cm V Hurdles at 0.5-metre intervals in a straight line.

Description
Player jumps forwards over each hurdle in quick succession until all the V Hurdles have been cleared, then walks back to the start and repeats the drill. See figure 2.8(a).

Key teaching points
- Use quick, rhythmic arm mechanics (see pages 45–47)
- Do not sink into the hips at the take-off and landing phases
- Land and take off from the balls of the feet
- Stand tall and look straight ahead
- Maintain control
- Start slowly and gradually build up speed

Sets and reps
2 sets of 6 reps, with a 1-minute recovery between each set.

Variations/progressions
- Perform lateral jumps – see figure 2.8(b)
- Perform jumps with a 180-degree twist – see figure 2.8(c)
- Use light hand weights; for the last rep of each of the sets, perform the drill without the weights as a contrast
- Perform two forward jumps and one back

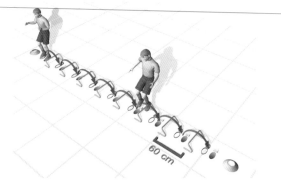

Figure 2.8(b) Multiple lateral jumps

Figure 2.8(a) Multiple jumps

Figure 2.8(c) Multiple jumps with a 180-degree twist

DRILL — RUNNING FORM – STRIDE FREQUENCY AND LENGTH

Aim
To practise the transfer from the acceleration phase to the increase in stride frequency and length required when running; to develop an efficient leg cycle, rhythm, power, foot placement, deceleration, control and balance.

Area/equipment
Indoor or outdoor area 35–55 metres long. Place 12 coloured Stride Frequency Canes, 1 metre in length, at different intervals flat on the ground in a straight line (the intervals will be determined by the size and age of the group you are working with).

Description
Starting 18 metres away from the first stick, the player accelerates towards the stick and, on reaching it, steps just over it. The player then continues with a measured stride frequency and length, as dictated by the sticks. On leaving the last stick or cane the player gradually decelerates. Return to the start and repeat the drill. See figure 2.9

Key teaching points
- Do not over-stride
- Work off the balls of the feet
- Try to develop and maintain a rhythm
- Keep the eyes and head up, as if you are looking over a fence
- Maintain correct running mechanics (see pages 48–62)
- Maintain an upright posture
- Stay focused

Sets and Reps
1 set of 4 reps.

Variations/progressions
- Set up the Stride Frequency Canes as shown in figure 2.9. The sticks now control the acceleration and deceleration phases
- Add a change of direction during the deceleration phase

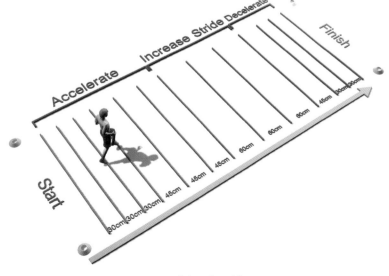

Figure 2.9 Stride length and frequency

DRILL   *RUNNING FORM – WITH A BALL*

Aim
To maintain good mechanics, balance and co-ordination while moving into position to play a shot; to improve decision-making ability.

Area/equipment
Indoor or outdoor area; ball. Place 8 V Hurdles at 0.5-metre intervals in a straight line. Place a Marker Spot at each end, approximately 2 metres away from the last hurdle.

Description
The coach stands at the end Marker Spot/cone with the ball. The player performs a mechanics drill through the hurdles and, on clearing the final hurdle, accelerates onto a ball that has been fed in at various angles by the coach. See figure 2.10(a).

Figure 2.10(a) Running form with a ball

Key teaching points
■ Maintain correct mechanics (see pages 34–41)
■ Stay focused by looking ahead
■ Fire the arms explosively when accelerating onto the ball

Sets and reps
3 sets of 6 reps. The sets should be made up of various mechanics drills.

Variations/progressions
■ On clearing the final hurdle, the ball is fed to the player at chest height. The player controls the ball and executes a side-foot volley to the coach, who lays the ball off for the player to accelerate on to. See figure 2.10(b)
■ The player performs lateral mechanic drills with his back to the coach; the coach also works laterally approximately 2 metres away from the player. The coach feeds the ball to the player, who must then turn to the left or right as instructed, then gather, control and return the ball. See figure 2.10(c)

Figure 2.10(b) Running form with a ball – variation 1

Figure 2.10(c) Running form with a ball – variation 2

DRILL

RUNNING FORM –
HURDLE MIRROR DRILLS

Aim
To improve the performance of mechanics under pressure; to improve random agility, dynamic balance and co-ordination.

Area/equipment
Indoor or outdoor area. Mark out a grid with 2 lines of 8 V Hurdles, with 0.5 metres between each hurdle and 2 metres between each line of hurdles.

Description
Players face each other while performing mechanics drills up and down the lines of hurdles. One player initiates the movements while the partner attempts to mirror those movements. The lead player can perform both lateral and linear mirror drills. See figure 2.11(a).

Key teaching points
■ Stay focused on your partner
■ The player mirroring should try to anticipate the lead player's movements
■ Maintain correct arm mechanics (see pages 45–47)

Sets and reps
Each player performs 3 sets of 30-second work periods, with a 30-second recovery between each work period.

Variations/progressions
■ First-to-the-ball drill – as above, except a ball is placed between the 2 lines of hurdles. The proactive partner commences the drill as normal then accelerates to the ball, collects it and dribbles to an end Marker Spot/cone. The reactive player attempts to beat the proactive player to the ball. See figure 2.11(b)
■ Lateral drills performed as above – players work in pairs with only 2 hurdles per player. These are great for improving short-stepping lateral marking skills. See figure 2.11(c)

Figure 2.11(b) First-to-the-ball hurdle mirror drills

Figure 2.11(c) Hurdle mirror drills with only
2 hurdles per player

Figure 2.11(a) Hurdle mirror drills

DRILL   RUNNING FORM – CURVED ANGLE RUN

Aim
To develop controlled, explosive fast feet while running on a curved angle.

Area/equipment
Indoor or outdoor area. Place 10 V Hurdles in a curved formation, 0.5 metres apart. Place a marker at each end, approximately 2 metres from the first and last hurdles respectively.

Description
Player performs running drills through the hurdles, such as the Dead-leg run, Lateral stepping or Leading leg run (see pages 48, 52 and 50 respectively). See figure 2.12.

Key teaching points
■ Work both left and right sides
■ The knee lift should be to no more than 45 degrees
■ Use short, sharp steps
■ Maintain powerful arm mechanics (see pages 45–47)
■ Maintain an upright posture
■ Look ahead at all times

Sets and reps
Each player performs 1 set of 6 reps, with a 30-second recovery between each rep

Variations/progressions
■ Introduce a ball for the player to pass while performing the drill or run on to at the end of the drill
■ Introduce tighter curves
■ Use immediately after straight run hurdle work

Figure 2.12 Curved angle run

DRILL   RUNNING FORM – COMPLEX MECHANICS

Aim

To prevent players reverting to bad habits, particularly when under pressure; to challenge players by placing them in match-like pressure situations; to maintain good running form even in the most difficult and demanding of situations.

Area/equipment

Indoor or outdoor area. Place 4 V Hurdles in a straight line with 0.5 metres between each hurdle. The next 4 V Hurdles are set slightly to one side, and the final 4 V Hurdles are placed back in line with the original 4.

Description

Player performs Dead-leg run (see page 48) over the hurdles with the dead leg changing over the 4 centre hurdles. Return to the start by performing the drill over the V Hurdles in the opposite direction. See figure 2.13(a).

Key teaching points

■ Maintain correct arm mechanics (see pages 45–47)
■ Work off the balls of the feet
■ Try to develop and maintain a rhythm
■ Keep the eyes and head up and look ahead
■ Maintain an upright posture
■ Keep the hips square

Sets and reps

4 sets of 4 reps.

Variations/progressions

■ Perform the drill laterally, moving both forwards and backwards to cross the centre 4 hurdles. See figure 2.13(b)
■ Place the hurdles in a cross formation and perform drills up to the centre and sideways, left or right, up or across
■ Introduce more players
■ When the drill has been mastered, players can accelerate out of the last hurdle on to a ball

Figure 2.13(a) Complex mechanics

Figure 2.13(b) Complex lateral mechanics

| DRILL | *RUNNING FORM –*
'THE SQUARE' COMPLEX MECHANICS |

Aim
To bring together running form drills in different combinations so that players become more comfortable at changing movement patterns when required.

Area/equipment
Indoor or outdoor area.

Description
Player performs a different mechanics drill down each line of hurdles until the square is completed. See figure 2.14.

Key teaching points
■ Maintain correct arm mechanics (see pages 45–47)
■ Work off the balls of the feet
■ Try to develop and maintain a rhythm
■ Keep the eyes and head up and look ahead
■ Maintain an upright posture
■ Keep the hips square

Sets and reps
4 sets of 4 reps.

Variation/progression
Vary the combination of drills.

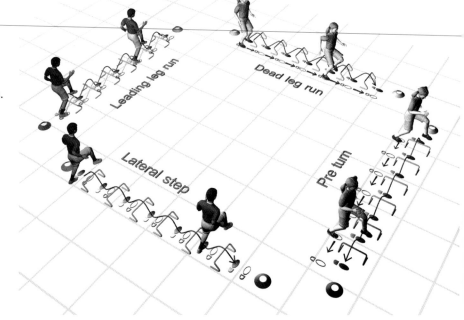

Figure 2.14 'The square' complex mechanics

DRILL

Aim
To develop football-specific speed endurance.

Area/equipment
Indoor or outdoor area. Place 8 Marker Spots in a 12-yard square and the remaining Marker Spots in the middle of the square.

Description
The centre dot is given the letter A. The other Marker Spots are placed approximately 6 yards away from the centre Marker Spot in a clock formation. The forward Marker Spot will be 12:00, forward right Marker Spot is 1:30, right Marker Spot is 3:00, back right Marker Spot is 4:30, back Marker Spot is 6:00, back left Marker Spot is 7:30, left Marker Spot is 9:00 and forward left Marker Spot is 10:30. See figure 2.15(a). Player performs interval runs as outlined below. For example, in the first set the player runs from A to 12:00, 12:00 to 10:30, 10:30 to A. This run equals approximately 18 yards. This equals 1 rep; 1 set of 5 reps equals 90 yards. The second set could be A to 6:00, 6:00 to 4:30, 4:30 to 1:30, 1:30 to A, A to 9:00, 9:00 to A. This rep is 42 yards; 1 set of 5 reps equals 210 yards.

Work:rest ratio (recovery between runs)
The work:rest ratio between each run will be as follows: 1:3, 1:2, etc. This means that if the run takes 8 seconds, the rest period will be either 3 or 2 times longer, i.e. 24 or 16 seconds. These times can be varied to increase the intensity of the work.

Recovery between sets
This is the recovery time between sets of runs.

Set one
5 x A to 12:00, 12:00 to 10:30, 10:30 to 9:00, 9:00 to A
Work:rest ratio: 1:3 pre-season, 1:2 in-season
Recovery between sets: 2 minutes
Total distance: 110 metres

Set two
5 x A to 6:00, 6:00 to 7:30, 7:30 to 4:30, 4:30 to A, A to 12:00, 12:00 to A
Work:rest ratio: 1:3 pre-season, 1:2 in-season
Recovery between sets: 2 minutes
Total distance: 190 metres

ENDURANCE TRAINING –
CLOCK ENDURANCE RUNS (Contd...)

Set three

5 x A to 9:00, 9:00 to 3:00, 3:00 to 4:30, 4:30 to 6:00, 6:00 to 12:00,
12:00 to A
Work:rest ratio: 1:3 pre-season, 1:2 in-season
Recovery between sets: 2 minutes
Total distance: 220 metres

Set four

6 x A to 10:30, 10:30 to 1:30, 1:30 to A, A to 7:30, 7:30 to 4:30,
4:30 to A, A to 12:00, 12:00 to A
Work:rest ratio: 1:3 pre-season, 1:2 in-season
Recovery between sets: 2 minutes
Total distance: 330 metres

Total session distance: 850 metres

Variations/progressions

- Perform runs with the ball
- Run in pairs
- Add codes for certain football-specific actions to be performed at certain parts of the clock, i.e. 12:00 = jump and head the ball; 6:00 = volley the ball, etc.
- Start with runs from different sections on the clock
- Vary the recovery time between sets
- Vary work:rest ratio
- Introduce an active recovery between runs (this can include ball skills)
- Run with hand weights
- Run with a weighted vest

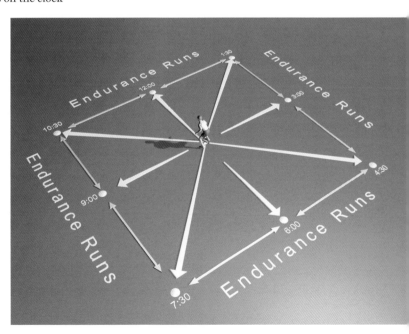

Figure 2.15 Clock endurance runs – set-up

DRILL *INTERVAL RUNNING SESSIONS*

Aim

To develop football-specific endurance.

Area/equipment

Indoor or outdoor area: Marker Spots set out at different distances as described in 'Sets and reps' below.

Description

Player runs at a medium to high intensity for the distances set out in 'Sets and reps' below. The work:rest ratio is calculated by the time taken to complete the run; for example, in session E, set 1 (10 x 20 m), if a single run takes you 5 seconds then you rest for 10 seconds before completing the second run, and so on. On completing the set of 10, you would take a 3-minute active recovery (walking before moving on to the second set of 5 x 50 m).

These interval runs are fantastic for developing endurance; they have a major impact on a player's VO_2 max without the need for running long, slow miles, and they also maintain a player's ability to be explosive, as they maintain fast-twitch fibres instead of recruiting slow-twitch fibres. Ensure that you warm up with 10 minutes of Dynamic Flex (see Chapter 1). Try to organise your training schedule so that you have at least 48 hours recovery between intense interval sessions.

Sets and reps

Session A

4 x 200 m
5 x 100 m
5 x 50 m
10 x 25 m
10 x 10 m

Work:rest ratio: 1:3
Recovery between sets: 3 minutes
For the 25 m and 10 m runs, players should start from different standing positions, e.g. backwards (turn to both shoulders) or sideways.
Total distance: 1900 m

Session B

5 x 250 m
5 x 150 m
5 x 100 m

Work:rest ratio: 1:3. The recovery between reps should be active (i.e. walking).
Recovery between sets: 3 minutes between sets 1 and 2; 2 minutes between sets 2 and 3
Total distance: 2500 m

ENDURANCE TRAINING –
INTERVAL RUNNING SESSIONS (Contd...)

Session C

10 x 75 m	Work:rest ratio of 1:3
10 x 50 m	Work:rest ratio of 1:3
10 x 30 m	Work:rest ratio of 1:2
10 x 20 m	Work:rest ratio of 1:2
20 x 5 m	Immediate turn around and repeat

Total distance: 1850 m

Session D

1 x 150 m
1 x 100 m
1 x 50 m
2 x 25 m
5 x 15 m
5 x 10 m

Work:rest ratio: 1:3
Players should complete session D five times with a full 3-minute recovery between each set.
Total distance: 2375 m

Session E

10 x 20 m	Work:rest ratio of 1:2
5 x 50 m	Work:rest ratio of 1:3
6 x 25 m	Work:rest ratio of 1:2
3 x 100 m	Work:rest ratio of 1:3
4 x 75 m	Work:rest ratio of 1:3
5 x 30 m	Work:rest ratio of 1:2
10 x 15 m	Work:rest ratio of 1:1.5

Recovery between sets: 3 minutes
Total distance: 1500 m

Session F

5 x 10 m	Work:rest ratio of 1:1.5
10 x 15 m	Work:rest ratio of 1:1.5
3 x 100 m	Work:rest ratio of 1:2.5
3 x 125 m	Work:rest ratio of 1:3
3 x 150 m	Work:rest ratio of 1:3
5 x 35 m	Work:rest ratio of 1:2
3 x 20 m	Work:rest ratio of 1:2

Recovery between sets: 3 minutes
Total distance: 1560 m

Session G

5 x 40 m	Work:rest ratio of 1:2
5 x 80 m	Work:rest ratio of 1:2.5
5 x 25 m	Work:rest ratio of 1:2
5 x 50 m	Work:rest ratio of 1:2
5 x 60 m	Work:rest ratio of 1:3
5 x 30 m	Work:rest ratio of 1:2
5 x 15 m	Work:rest ratio of 1:2

Recovery between sets: 3 minutes
Total distance: 1500 m

Variations/progressions
- Use different starting positions
- Set the markers out at different angles

SPEED ENDURANCE TRAINING –
DRILL INTERVAL RUNNING SESSIONS

Aim

To develop a player's ability to recover and repeat short, explosive bursts of activity.

Area/equipment

Indoor or outdoor area; Marker Spots set out at different distances, as described in 'Sets and reps' below.

Description

Player performs high-intensity runs as described in 'Sets and reps' below.

Sets and reps

Session A

    5 x 80 m
    5 x 25 m
    5 x 50 m
    5 x 60 m
    5 x 30 m

Work:rest ratio: 1:2
Recovery between sets: 3 minutes

Session B

6 x 40 m	Work:rest ratio of 1:2
6 x 50 m	Work:rest ratio of 1:2
6 x 30 m	Work:rest ratio of 1:2
6 x 20 m	Work:rest ratio of 1:2
20 x 5 m	Immediate turn around and repeat

Recovery between sets: 3 minutes

Session C

5 x 50 m	Work:rest ratio of 1:2
5 x 80 m	Forwards for 40 m, backwards for 10 m and then forwards for 30 m. Work:rest ratio of 1:2.5
5 x 40 m	Work:rest ratio of 1:2
5 x 80 m	Forwards for 40 m, backwards for 10 m and then forwards for 30 m. Work:rest ratio of 1:2.5
5 x 50 m	Work:rest ratio of 1:2

Recovery between sets: 3 minutes

SPEED ENDURANCE TRAINING –
INTERVAL RUNNING SESSIONS (Contd...)

Session D

6 x 40 m	Forwards for 20 m, turn and run for 10 m, turn again and run for 10 m
8 x 20 m	To be completed from different start positions.
6 x 40 m	As set 1
8 x 20 m	As set 2
6 x 30 m	Forwards for 10 m, backwards for 10 m and then forwards for 10 m

Work:rest ratio of 1:2

Recovery between sets: 3 minutes

Sets 2 and 4 should be completed from different starting positions, which you should select from the variations and progressions below. Be sure to vary them within the set and from session to session.

Variations/progressions

Use the following starting positions:

■ Forward split stance – be sure to alternate the leading leg

■ Forward parallel stance – again, be sure to alternate the foot that makes the fist step

■ Sideways stance – turn and go, bearing the above point in mind

■ Backwards stance – turn and go, turning on alternate shoulders

CHAPTER 3 INNERVATION

FAST FEET, AGILITY, CO-ORDINATION, DYNAMIC BALANCE AND CONTROL FOR FOOTBALL

Football places incredible demands on a player's ability to move quickly in all directions; to change direction, decelerate, stop instantly and start again, jump into the air, land and instantly move off in another direction, all the time maintaining balance and control in order to hit the ball with efficient and effective power. This complex sequence of movements can be practised and perfected during the innervation stage of the SAQ Continuum.

Innervation is the transition stage from warm-up and mechanics to periods of high-intensity work that activate the neural pathways. Using Fast Foot™ Ladders, dance-like patterns such as twists, jumps and turns are all introduced, increasing the rate of firing in the neuromuscular system.

Once the basic footwork patterns have been mastered, more advanced, football-specific footwork drills that require speed, co-ordination, agility and dynamic balance can be introduced. The key here is to speed up the movement techniques without compromising the quality of the player's mechanics. The drills in this chapter progress from simple footwork patterns to complex football-specific drills that incorporate group and ball work that also include body awareness and visual development.

DRILL   *FAST FOOT LADDER – SINGLE RUN*

Aim
To develop fast feet with control, precision and power.

Area/equipment
Indoor or outdoor area; Fast Foot Ladder (ensure that this is the correct ladder for the type of surface being used).

Description
Player covers the length of the ladder by placing a foot in each ladder space, then returns to the start by jogging back beside the ladder. See figure 3.1(a).

Key teaching points
■ Maintain correct running form/mechanics (see pages 48–62)
■ Start slowly and gradually increase the speed
■ Maintain an upright posture
■ Stress that quality, not quantity, is important

Sets and reps
3 sets of 4 reps, with a 1-minute recovery between each set.

Variations/progressions
■ Single lateral step – as above, but performed laterally. See figure 3.1(b)
■ In and out – move sideways along the ladder, stepping into and out of each ladder space, i.e. both feet in and both feet out. See figure 3.1(c)
■ 'Icky shuffle' – side-stepping movement into and out of each ladder space while moving forwards. See figure 3.1(d)
■ Double run – perform as single run above, but with both feet in each ladder space. See figure 3.1(e)
■ Hopscotch – see figure 3.1(f)
■ Single-space jumps – two-footed jumps into and out of each ladder space. See figure 3.1(g)
■ Two forwards and one back – see figure 3.1(h)
■ 'Spotty dogs' – see figure 3.1(i)
■ 'Twist again' – see figure 3.1(j)
■ Hops in and out – see figure 3.1(k)
■ Carioca – see figure 3.1(l)

FAST FOOT LADDER – SINGLE RUN (Contd...)

Figure 3.1(a) Fast Foot Ladder – single run

Figure 3.1(b) Fast Foot Ladder – single lateral step

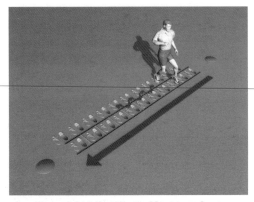

Figure 3.1(c) Fast Foot Ladder – in and out

Figure 3.1(d) Fast Foot Ladder – 'icky shuffle'

Figure 3.1(e) Fast Foot Ladder – double run

Figure 3.1(f) Fast Foot Ladder – hopscotch

FAST FOOT LADDER – SINGLE RUN (Contd...)

Figure 3.1(g) Fast Foot Ladder – single-space jumps

Figure 3.1(h) Fast Foot Ladder – two forwards
and one back

Figure 3.1(i) Fast Foot Ladder – 'spotty dogs'

Figure 3.1(j) Fast Foot Ladder – 'twist again'

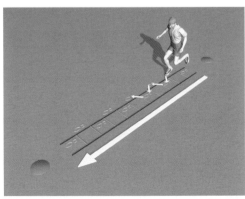

Figure 3.1(k) Fast Foot Ladder– hops in and out

Figure 3.1(l) Fast Foot Ladder – carioca

DRILL | FAST FOOT LADDER – FORWARD STEP

Aim

To develop a fast, controlled first forward step, with the lead foot in the direction of the oncoming ball.

Area/equipment

Indoor or outdoor area; Fast Foot Ladder (ensure that this is the correct ladder for the type of surface being used); 4 different-coloured Marker Spots.

Description

Put the ladder on the ground and place a coloured Marker Spot in each of the ladder squares (in a 7.5-foot ladder there are 4 squares) as follows: a blue marker in the far left box, a red centre-left, a yellow marker centre-right and a green marker far right. The player stands in a lateral position facing the ladder opposite the red and yellow marker dots. The drill commences with the player shuffling on the spot; the coach then randomly calls a colour and the player has to move his or her opposite foot across and jab the nominated coloured marker, then return immediately to the centre position ready for the next call. Therefore, the left foot will forward step to the green and yellow markers while the right foot will forward step to the red and blue markers. See figure 3.2.

Key teaching points

- Maintain an athletic position
- Maintain correct form/mechanics
- Use short steps and work on the balls of the feet
- Keep off the heels
- Do not sink into the hips

Sets and reps

5 sets of 1 minute, with a 1-minute recovery between sets.

Variation/Progression

Coach to throw a ball in front of the square nominated for the player to return.

Figure 3.2 Fast Foot Ladder – forward step

DRILL   *FAST FOOT LADDER – 'T' FORMATION*

Aim

To develop speed of acceleration when pressing the opposition; to develop controlled lateral cross cover and defensive backwards jockeying movements.

Area/equipment

Indoor or outdoor area. Place 2 ladders in a 'T' formation with 3 Marker Spots at the end of each ladder.

Description

The player accelerates down the ladder using single steps. On reaching the second ladder, the player moves laterally either left or right using short lateral steps. On coming out of the ladder, the player jockeys backwards toward the start line. See figure 3.3.

Key teaching points

■ Maintain correct running form/mechanics (see pages 48–62)
■ Use a strong arm drive when transferring from linear to lateral steps
■ When jockeying backwards, keep the head and eyes up

Sets and reps

3 sets of 4 reps, 2 moving to the left and 2 moving to the right, with a 1-minute recovery between each set

Variations/progressions

■ Start with a lateral run and, upon reaching the end ladder, accelerate in a straight line forwards down the ladder. On reaching the end, turn and accelerate back towards the starting line
■ Coach stands 5–6 metres away from the head of the T and, while the player is moving laterally through the ladder, delivers a ball for the player to return
■ Mix and match the fast-foot ladder drills described earlier (see pages 71–4)
■ Use mannequins for players to press

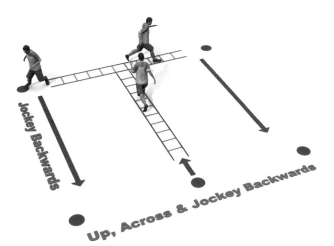

Figure 3.3 Fast Foot Ladder – 'T' formation

DRILL FAST FOOT LADDER – CROSSOVER

Aim
To develop speed, agility and change of direction in a more football-specific 'crowded' area; to improve reaction time, peripheral vision and timing.

Area/equipment
Large indoor or outdoor area. Place 4 ladders in a cross formation, leaving a clear centre space of approximately 3 square yards. Place a Marker Spot 1 metre from the start of each ladder.

Description
Label the ladders A, B, C and D. Players line up at the start of each ladder. Simultaneously, the players at the head of each line accelerate down the ladder performing a single-step drill; on reaching the end of the ladder, they accelerate across the centre square and join the end of the queue. They do not travel down the second ladder! See figure 3.4.

Key teaching points
■ Maintain correct running form/mechanics (see pages 48–62)
■ Keep the head and eyes up and be aware of other players, particularly around the centre area

Sets and reps
3 sets of 6 reps, with a 1-minute recovery between each set.

Variations/progressions
■ At the end of the first ladder, side-step to the right or left and single-step down the appropriate adjacent ladder
■ Vary the fast-foot ladder drills performed down the first ladder
■ Include a 360-degree turn in the centre square; this helps to develop body and positional awareness
■ Introduce a ball into the middle of the grid. Players accelerate out of the ladder on to the ball and touch pass to each other

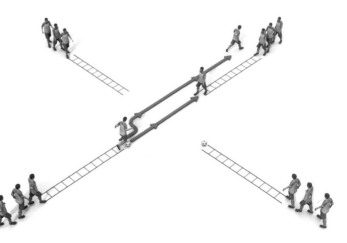

Figure 3.4 Fast Foot Ladder – crossover

| DRILL | FAST FOOT LADDER – MOVE AND PASS |

Aim
To develop fast feet, dynamic balance, co-ordination, speed and agility while moving into position to strike a ball.

Area/equipment
Large indoor or outdoor area. Place a 2-metre ladder on the ground with a marker dot about 1 metre away from each end.

Description
Player 1 performs fast foot drills down the ladder either laterally or linearly; Player 2, standing 2 metres away from the ladder in a central position, feeds the ball into him at different heights, requiring the first player to perform either a foot, chest or head skill to control and return the ball. See figure 3.5.

Key teaching points
■ Concentrate on good footwork patterns
■ Ensure that correct technical skills are used when controlling and returning the ball
■ Ensure that the player performing the drill returns to correct running form/mechanics after returning the ball

Sets and reps
3 sets of 6 reps, with a 1-minute recovery between each set.

Variations/progressions
■ Vary the fast-foot drills performed by Player 1
■ Use a 5-metre ladder

Figure 3.5 Fast Foot Ladder – move and pass

DRILL

FAST FOOT LADDER COMBINATION DRILLS – MOVE AND PASS

Aim
To develop fast feet, dynamic balance, co-ordination, speed and agility while incorporating football-specific ball control and passing combination drills.

Area/equipment
Large indoor or outdoor area. Place two ladders in an upside-down 'L' pattern, with two more mirroring this formation approximately 2 metres away. Place Marker Spots at the start and end of each 'L' (1 metre away from the end of the ladders). Place another 2 Marker Spots 5 metres away and 1 metre apart, in line with the centre space. Place a ball at the end of one ladder.

Description
Two players, one on each 'L' pattern, start with linear fast-foot drills, then transfer to lateral drills as the ladders dictate. Player 1 accelerates on to the ball and dribbles for 2 metres before passing the ball for Player 2 to move on to. On receiving the ball Player 2 takes just one or two touches before passing the ball back to Player 1, who shoots the ball through the Marker Spots. The players then jog back to the start, where they swap roles. See figure 3.6.

Key teaching points
■ Maintain correct running form/mechanics (see pages 48–62)
■ Ensure that correct technical skills are used when players are on the ball
■ Encourage the players to use clear communication – visual and audio

Sets and reps
3 sets of 6 reps (i.e. 3 reps as Player 1 and 3 reps as Player 2), with a 1-minute recovery between each set

Variation/progression
Vary the Fast Foot Ladder drills performed linearly and laterally by the players.

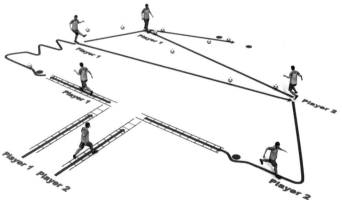

Figure 3.6 Fast Foot Ladder combination drills – move and pass

DRILL | *FAST FOOT LADDER –* *'IPSWICH TOWN' GRID*

Aim
To develop fast feet, agility and control in a restricted area while under pressure from other players.

Area/equipment
Large indoor or outdoor area. Place 4 ladders side by side

Description
Working in pairs, players perform fast-foot drills while covering the length of the outside ladders. On the coach's signal the players move to the inside ladders, thus working side by side. On reaching the end they jog back to the start line. See figure 3.7(a).

Key teaching points
■ Maintain correct running form/mechanics (see pages 48–62)
■ Encourage the players to push and nudge each other to simulate the close-marking situations that occur in a game
■ If players are 'knocked' off-balance, ensure that they re-assert the correct arm mechanics as soon as possible

Sets and reps
3 sets of 4 reps, with a 1-minute recovery between each set.

Variations/progressions
■ Start players on the central ladders and work them out and back in
■ Start players on ladders next to each other on either the left or right of the grid, and work them across the 4 ladders. See figure 3.7(b)

Figure 3.7(a) Fast foot ladder – 'Ipswich Town' grid

Figure 3.7(b) Fast Foot Ladder – 'Ipswich Town' grid – variation

DRILL   *FAST FOOT LADDER – GIANT CROSSOVER*

Aim
To develop fast feet, speed, agility, dynamic balance, co-ordination, peripheral vision and reaction time when playing shots.

Area/equipment
Large indoor or outdoor area. Place 4 ladders in a cross formation with 22 metres between them in the centre area. Place a ball at the end of one ladder and another at the end of an adjacent ladder.

Description
Split the squad into 4 equal groups and place them at the start of each ladder. Players accelerate down the ladders, performing fast foot drills. Two players will have a ball at the end of their respective ladders; they dribble the ball across the centre area and pass it to the oncoming player, who receives and controls the ball before passing it on to the next oncoming player. Having passed the ball, the player runs to the start of the queue on the opposite side of the cross. Do not travel down this ladder! See figure 3.8.

Key teaching points
■ This should be a continuous drill
■ Maintain correct running form/mechanics (see pages 48–62)
■ Correct technical skills must be used when players are on the ball
■ Players should use clear communication

Sets and reps
3 sets of 6 reps, with a 1-minute recovery between each set

Variations/progressions
■ Vary the passing skills used in the centre area
■ Vary the amount of control allowed, e.g. one touch , two touch, etc.

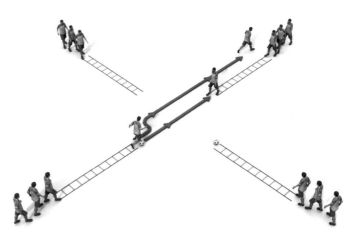

Figure 3.8 Fast Foot Ladder – giant crossover

DRILL FAST FOOT LADDER – LONG PASS

Aim
To develop fast feet, speed, agility and acceleration while focusing on getting into position early to receive a long pass; to develop accurate passing over long distances.

Area/equipment
Large indoor or outdoor area. Place 2 ladders next to each other, 10 metres (10 yards) apart. Another 2 ladders should be placed in the same formation, 35–45 metres (40–50 yards) away. Place a ball at the end of each of the first 2 ladders.

Description
Split the squad into 4 equal groups and place them at the ends of each ladder so all players are facing the centre space. Players perform nominated fast-foot drills down the ladders. Two players collect the balls at the end of their ladders and make long, diagonal or straight passes to the players coming down the opposite ladders. On completing the passes, the players jockey backwards to their start positions. See figure 3.9.

Key teaching points
■ Maintain correct running form/mechanics (see pages 48–62)
■ Correct technical skills must be used when players are on the ball
■ The timing of the player who is to receive the ball is crucial – he should receive the ball just as he leaves the ladder to enter the centre space
■ The player receiving the ball should do so on the move, *not* standing still

Sets and reps
3 sets of 6 reps, with a 1-minute recovery between each set.

Variations/progressions
■ Make the long pass a diagonal pass to the oncoming player on the other set of ladders
■ For sprint endurance conditioning, make the players accelerate across the centre space to join the start of the ladder diagonally opposite them

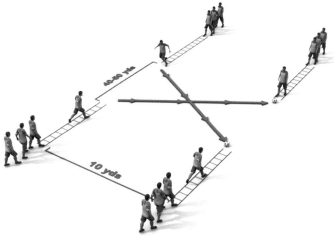

Figure 3.9 Fast Foot Ladder – long pass

DRILL   FAST FOOT LADDER – PRESSING DRILL

Aim
To develop explosive group pressing skills.

Area/equipment
Large indoor or outdoor area. Place 4 Fast Foot Ladders in a cross formation, with a Marker Spot 1 metre from the start of each ladder.

Description
Split the squad into 4 equal groups and place them at the start of each ladder. Simultaneously, the first 4 players, 1 from each group, accelerate down the ladders and explode into the middle, decelerating as they come into the centre space. When they are within touching distance, the press is called, and the players now jockey backwards clockwise between the ladder they have run down and the next ladder. They now join the group at the start of the next ladder, ready to repeat the drill. See figure 3.10.

Key teaching points
- Maintain correct running form/mechanics (see pages 48–62)
- Keep the head and eyes up and be aware of other players, particularly around the centre area
- Encourage players to communicate with each other when accelerating into the middle

Sets and reps
1 set equals 2 minutes of continuous work; perform 3 sets with a 1-minute recovery between each set

Variations/progressions
- Vary the drills performed by the players down the ladders
- Instead of jockeying backwards, players turn and explode back
- Work both clockwise and anti-clockwise

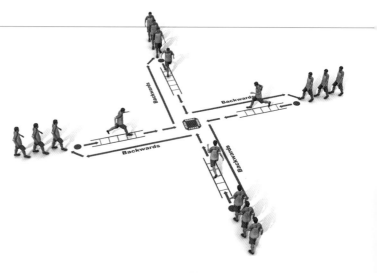

Figure 3.10 Fast Foot Ladder – pressing drill

| DRILL | *FAST FOOT LADDER – CLOCK DRILL* |

Aim

To develop speed, agility, change of direction, acceleration and deceleration skills; to improve decision-making and reaction times.

Area/equipment

Large indoor or outdoor area; 2 sets of four-piece Fast Foot Ladders (8 pieces total) – ensure that the correct ladders are used for the type of surface; 8 Marker Spots or cones. Place the ladders in a clock formation. The times to be represented are 12:00, 1:30, 3:00, 4:30, 6:00, 7:30, 9:00 and 10:30. The centre space should be 5 yards square. Place the Marker Spots or cones outside the grid, 3 yards from the end of each ladder.

Description

Players are grouped at the centre of the clock. Each player is allocated a number. The drill commences with the players jogging around in the centre space. The coach calls a number and then a time on the clock. That player then accelerates into position and down the nominated ladder, around the outside Marker Spot/cone and then returns to the centre. See figure 3.11.

Key teaching points

- Maintain correct running form/mechanics (see pages 48–62)
- Keep the head and eyes up and be aware of other players

Sets and reps

1 set equals 2 minutes of continuous work; perform 3 sets with a 1-minute recovery between each set

Variations/progressions

- Allocate two players the same number; these players then have to compete to see who can get down the ladder first
- Introduce ball work in the centre area

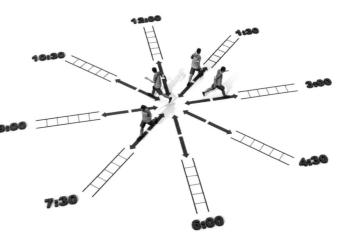

Figure 3.11 Fast Foot Ladder – clock drill

DRILL   LINE DRILLS

Aim
To develop quick feet.

Area/equipment
Indoor or outdoor area. Use any line marked on the ground surface.

Description
Players perform single split steps over the line and back. See figure 3.12(a).

Figure 3.12(b) Line drills – two-footed jumps

Key teaching points
■ Maintain good arm mechanics (see pages 45–47)
■ Maintain an upright posture
■ Maintain a strong core
■ Try to develop a rhythm
■ Keep the head and eyes up

Sets and reps
3 sets of 20 reps, with a 1-minute recovery between each set.

Variations/progressions
■ Two-footed jumps over the line and back – see figure 3.12(b)
■ Stand astride the line and bring the feet in to touch the line before moving them out again. Perform the drill as quickly as possible. See figure 3.12(c)
■ Two-footed side jumps over the line and back
■ Two-footed side jumps with a 180-degree twist in the air over the line and back – see figure 3.12(d)
■ Single quick hops
■ Complex variation: introduce the ball either at the end of the drill for the player to explode on to and return, or during the drill for the player to return before continuing

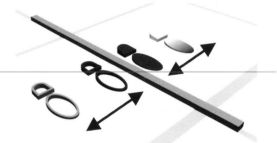

Figure 3.12(c) Line drills – astride the line

Figure 3.12(a) Line drills – single split steps

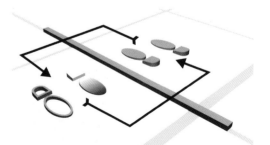

Figure 3.12(d) Line drills – two-footed side jumps with a 180-degree twist

DRILL QUICK BOX STEPS AND JUMPS

Aim
To develop explosive power and control. (N.B. The emphasis is on speed.)

Area/equipment
Indoor or outdoor area; a bench, aerobics step or suitable strong box with a non-slip surface, about 30 cm high.

Figure 3.13(b) Quick box steps and jumps – two-footed jumps

Description
Player performs an alternated split step jump on the box, i.e. one foot on the box and one on the floor. See figure 3.13(a).

Key teaching points
■ Practise the drill slowly first to perfect balance and the foot placement, then gradually build up speed
■ Focus on good arm drive
■ Maintain an upright posture
■ Maintain a strong core
■ Keep the head and eyes up
■ Work off the balls of the feet
■ Work at a high level of intensity once technique is perfected
■ Try to develop a rhythm

Figure 3.13(c) Quick box steps and jumps – two-footed side jumps

Figure 3.13(d) Quick box steps and jumps – straddle jumps

Sets and reps
3 sets of 20 reps, with a 1-minute recovery between each set.

Variations/progressions
■ Two-footed jumps on and off the box – see figure 3.13(b)
■ Two-footed side jumps on and off the box – see figure 3.13(c)
■ Straddle jumps – see figure 3.13(d)
■ Hops on and off the box (10 reps leading with the left foot and 10 leading with the right foot) – see figure 3.13(e)
■ Alternate hops – hop onto the box, landing on the opposite foot. Take off to land on the other side of the box, again on the opposite foot. See figure 3.13(f)

Figure 3.13(e) Quick box steps and jumps – hops

Figure 3.13(a) Quick box steps and jumps – alternated split step

Figure 3.13(f) Quick box steps and jumps – alternate hops

DRILL   FEET–EYE CO-ORDINATION DEVELOPMENT

Aim
To develop lightning-fast feet, and feet–eye co-ordination (hand–eye co-ordination is involved when working with goalkeepers).

Area/equipment
Indoor or outdoor area; Sidestrike; ball.

Description
Player performs lateral footwork patterns on the Sidestrike. When the drill has been perfected, the ball is introduced for the player to return. See figure 3.14.

Key teaching points
■ Work off the balls of the feet
■ Maintain a strong core
■ Keep the hips square
■ Develop a rhythm
■ Use correct catching and throwing techniques

Sets and Reps
5 sets of 30 seconds with a 45-second recovery between sets and a 3-minute recovery after all sets have been completed. N.B. this is a very high-intensity drill.

Variations/progressions
■ Perform forward steps
■ Perform crossover steps
■ Introduce the ball for the player to return
■ Work with a partner who stands 5 yards in front of the Sidestrike and randomly drops the ball for the player to explode on to
■ With goalkeepers, throw the ball for them to catch and return

Figure 3.14 Feet–eye co-ordination development

CHAPTER 4 ACCUMULATION OF POTENTIAL

This part of the SAQ Continuum brings together the areas of work already practised. Many of the mechanics and fast feet drills develop a specific skill; however, in football these different skills are rarely isolated but rather occur in quick succession or in combinations. An example of this is when a player, after heading the ball away in a defensive position, then runs to close down an opponent in a dangerous position to ensure a counter-attack is broken down. If the ball is then lobbed over him by an opponent, the player needs to turn explosively and accelerate back to chase the ball. Combinations of manoeuvres occur over different time-spans throughout a game of football. Research has confirmed that phases of play during a football match usually last for an average of 20 seconds [Personal communication. Consultation. Premiership club performance analysis 2003, 2006].

This indicates that the movements being used are short and very explosive. Ladders, hurdles, mannequins, marker dots, spiked poles, balls and so on can be used in football-specific circuits to develop programmed agility and condition the player for this type of high-intensity, multi-directional work.

The SAQ football-specific circuit is also an excellent time for the manager, coach or trainer to assess the quality of movement being used. If technique deteriorates at any time within the circuit, more time needs to be spent on the mechanics and innervation stages.

This phase should not fatigue players. Plan for high-intensity, high-quality movement rather than a high quantity of sets and reps, and ensure a maximum recovery period between sets and reps. Quality, not quantity, is the key here.

DRILL | AGILITY RUNS – T-RUN

Aim
To develop football-specific speed and agility.

Area/equipment
A large indoor or outdoor area. Place 4 Spiked Poles or Marker Spots 5 metres (5 yards) apart in a 'T' formation. See figure 4.1(a).

Description
The player starts on the left-hand side of the first Spiked Poles and accelerates to the Spiked Pole directly ahead. He then passes around this Spiked Pole and turns to his right before accelerating on to the end Spiked Pole (see figure 4.1(b)). The player then runs around the end Spiked Pole and returns to the middle Spiked Pole before finishing at the opposite side of the start position. Repeat the drill by starting on the right of the first Spiked Pole and turning to the left at the middle Spiked Pole (see figure 4.1(c)).

Key teaching points
- Maintain correct running form/mechanics (see pages 48–62)
- Work on shortening the steps used in the turn
- Focus on increasing the speed of the arm drive when coming out of the turns
- Ensure that players work their weak sides – most players will have a preferred turning side

Sets and reps
3 sets of 5 reps, with a 30-second recovery between each rep and a 1-minute recovery between each set.

Variation/progression
The coach stands at the centre Marker Spot/cone. The player accelerates towards the coach, who provides a signal – verbal or visual – to dictate which way the player turns.

Figure 4.1(b) T-run – step 1

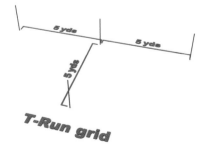

Figure 4.1(a) T-run – setup

Figure 4.1(c) T-run – step 2

| DRILL | *AGILITY RUNS –* *SWERVE DEVELOPMENT RUNS* |

Aim

To develop fine-angle running at pace, as if trying to lose a close marker or create space to receive a ball.

Area/equipment

A large indoor or outdoor area. Set out 8–12 Spiked Poles, Marker Spots or cones in a zigzag formation. The distance between the Spiked Poles/Marker Spots/cones should be 2–4 metres at varying angles (this will make the runs more realistic). The total length of the run will be 22–25 metres.

Description

The player accelerates from the first Spiked Pole/Marker Spot/cone and swerves around the outside of all of the others to complete the course. The player gently jogs back to the starting Spiked Pole before repeating the drill. See figure 4.2(a).

Key teaching points

- Maintain correct running form/mechanics (see pages 48–62)
- Work on shortening the steps used in the turn
- Focus on increasing the speed of the arm drive when coming out of the turns.
- Ensure that players take the tightest possible angles around the Marker Spots
- Keep the head and eyes up

Sets and reps

3 sets of 5 reps, with a 30-second recovery between each rep and a 1-minute recovery between each set.

Variations/progressions

- Use light hand weights for the first 4 reps, then perform the last rep without the weights as a contrast
- Tighten the angles by getting the player to zigzag inside the grid, running from the inside of each Spiked Pole

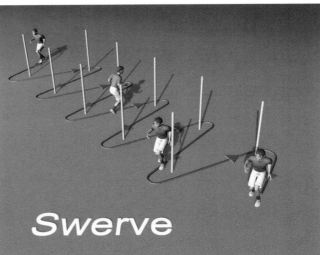

Figure 4.2 Swerve development runs

DRILL | *FOUR-TURN, FOUR-ANGLE RUN*

Aim

To develop turns and angled changes of direction with control, balance and co-ordination.

Area/equipment

A large indoor or outdoor area. Place 5 Marker Spots, cones or Spiked Poles in a cross formation with a centre Marker Spot or cone. The points of the cross are equally spaced out 5 yards from the centre. Label the Marker Spots/cones/poles A, B, C and D; the centre marker/cone is E.

Description

Player starts at centre marker E, runs around Marker Spot/cone A and back to E, changes angle to run around B and back to E, and so on around C and D. See figure 4.3(a).

Key teaching point

Ensure that correct movement mechanics are maintained (see pages 34–41).

Sets and reps

2 sets of 2 reps, with a 1-minute recovery between each set and a 2-minute recovery between each rep.

Variation/progression

Add 2 or 3 additional Marker Spots/cones between centre Marker Spot/cone E and Marker Spot/cones B and D. The player has to swerve in between the Marker Spots, out and back.

Figure 4.3 Four-turn, four-angle run

DRILL   *COMBINATION RUNS*

Aim

To develop a combination of running and movement patterns that will help develop players' gross motor skills.

Area/equipment

A large indoor or outdoor area, depending on space available. Place hurdles, Fast Foot Ladders, Spiked Poles and Marker Spots/cones in different formations and combinations. See figures 4.4(a) and (b).

Description

Player completes the circuit by performing different drills/skills, e.g. stepping, jumping, swerving, etc.

Key teaching points

Maintain correct movement running form/mechanics for all activities (see pages 48–62).

Sets and reps

2 sets of 2 reps, with a 1-minute recovery between each set and a 2-minute recovery between each rep.

Variations/progressions

◼ Vary the drills at hurdles, ladders, etc
◼ Set out identical circuits and introduce team relays

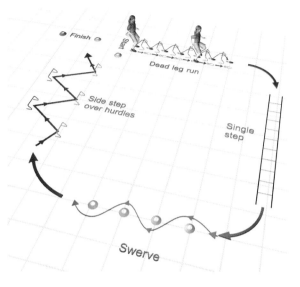

Figure 4.4(a) Combination runs – circuit 1

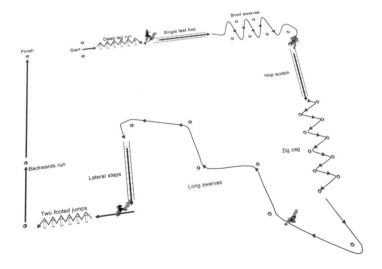

Figure 4.4(b) Combination runs – circuit 2

DRILL TEAM COMBINATION RUNS

Aim
To develop multi-directional movement, balance, co-ordination and body control while competing against another team.

Area/equipment
A large indoor or outdoor area. Place 2 or more identical sets of hurdles, Fast Foot Ladders, Marker Spots, Spiked Poles and Marker Spot/cones next to each other. Ensure there is a starting and finishing point for the teams. See figure 4.5 for circuit ideas.

Description
Teams complete the circuit performing different drills/skills, e.g. stepping, jumping, swerving, etc, competing against each other. The team that finishes first or incurs fewest errors is the winner.

Key teaching points
- Maintain correct running form/mechanics for all activities (see pages 48–62)
- Ensure that quality of movement is not sacrificed for speed

Sets and reps
2 sets of 2 reps, with a 1-minute recovery between each set and a 2-minute recovery between each rep.

Variations/progressions
- Vary the drills at hurdles, ladders, etc
- Introduce team relays

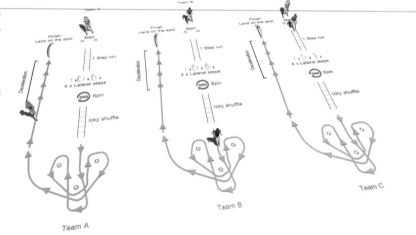

Figure 4.5 Team combination runs

DRILL *CONDITIONING CIRCUIT*

Aim

To improve general health and fitness, including cardiovascular health, balance, agility, co-ordination, reactions, manipulation and visual skills; to be challenged and have fun at the same time.

Area/equipment

A large indoor or outdoor area with Marker Spots, hurdles, ladders, agility discs and Jelly Balls or footballs. Set out the equipment at different stations so that different drills can be performed. See figure 4.6.

Description

Players perform drills at each station for an allocated time, then move to the next station in the circuit to perform the next drill.

Key teaching points

- Use the correct techniques required for each station, i.e. correct arm mechanics, posture, etc.
- Ensure that all drills are demonstrated prior to warming up
- Provide constant feedback to all players during the circuit

Sets and reps

1 circuit includes 40 seconds per station with a 25-second changeover.

Variation/progression

Add different drills at each station.

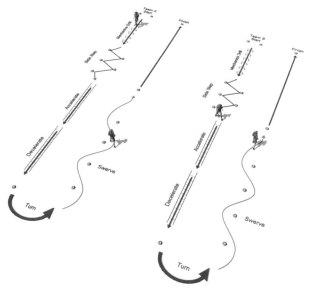

Figure 4.6 Conditioning drill

DRILL MULTI-PLAYER PRESSING DRILL

Aim
To develop acceleration, deceleration, teamwork and communication in closing down space on opponents.

Area/equipment
Large indoor or outdoor area, 12 Mannequins, 8 Spiked Poles, 4 Marker Spots or cones and 4 Fast Foot Ladders. Set out the equipment in a circuit, as shown in figure 4.7. (Spiked Poles can be used instead of the Mannequins; Marker Spots or cones can be used to set out the whole circuit.)

Description
Players line up in groups of 4 opposite the starter Marker Spots or cones. They accelerate in line together around the first Spiked Pole, down the ladders and then press the first line of Mannequins. The press position is held for no longer than 2–3 seconds. Players now accelerate around the Mannequins and repeat the press on the next line of mannequins. Repeat this on the third line of Mannequins. Players then accelerate around the Mannequins and perform swerve runs through the Spiked Poles, then decelerate and jog back to the finishing line.

Key teaching points
- Ensure that correct movement mechanics are maintained (see pages 34–41)
- Encourage players to communicate so that a line is maintained when they press the Mannequins
- Ensure that deceleration techniques are sound

Sets and reps
1 set of 5 reps, with a 1-minute recovery between each rep.

Variations/progressions
- Vary the angles of the second and third lines of Mannequins
- Introduce backward running after completing the swerve runs

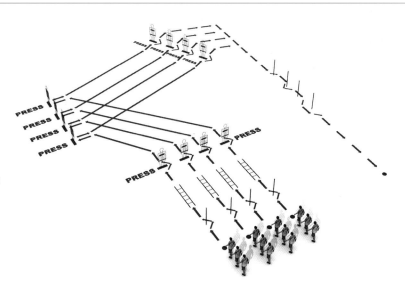

Figure 4.7 Multi-player team pressing drill

DRILL FOOTBALL-SPECIFIC CIRCUIT

Aim
To develop a range of creative football-specific running patterns likely to be encountered in games in order to enhance players' skill base and keep them motivated and challenged.

Area/equipment
Half a football pitch with Marker Spots, hurdles, Fast Foot Ladders, Spiked Poles and balls placed in a circuit within the area.

Description
Players follow the circuit, which takes them through Fast Foot Ladders, over hurdles, side-stepping through Marker Spots, running backwards, jumping, turning and performing ball skills – see figure 4.8. One circuit should take players 30–60 seconds to complete.

Key teaching points
Maintain correct running form/mechanics for all activities (see pages 48–62).

Sets and reps
1 set of 6 reps with a varied recovery time between each rep, depending on the stage in the season.

Variation/progression
The coach should use his imagination to add, subtract and vary the drills within the circuit. This will keep players motivated and challenged.

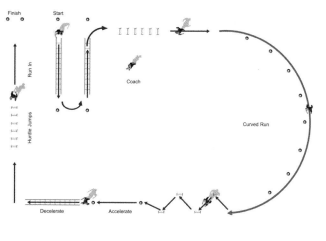

Figure 4.8 Football-specific circuit

THREE-STEP, MULTI-DIRECTIONAL ACCELERATION FOR FOOTBALL

The exercises outlined in this chapter have been designed to boost response times and develop multi-directional, explosive movements. Programmable and random agility are trained using resisted and assisted high-quality plyometrics. Plyometrics exercises focus on the stretch–shortening cycle of the muscles involved, an action that is a central part of football performance. Plyometrics drills include drop-jumps, hops, skips and bounds. Plyometrics can be fun and challenging and adds variety to training sessions; however, there is potential for injury with these exercises so they must be performed using the correct technique and at the correct point in the training session.

Upper-body speed and power are catered for with jelly ball workouts, which develop the kind of strength required for holding off an opponent. These workouts also develop the power used to develop arm drive and improve running speed; jumping height can be dramatically improved.

SAQ utilises different types of resistance techniques including static, mobile and flexi-cord resistance. Elastic resistance exercise has been used for almost a century and has been shown to improve strength, power and function in a wide range of people, from elite athletes to young and older population groups (Philip Page, Todd S. Ellenbecker, 2003).

The crucial element of explosive drills is the implementation of the 'contrast' phase. This simply means performing the drill without resistance for one or two reps immediately after performing it with resistance. The non-resisted movements will naturally be more explosive and more easily remembered and reproduced over a period of time.

The key here is to ensure that quality, not quantity, is the priority. Efforts must be carefully monitored – this is a time for high-intensity explosive action, not 'tongue-hanging out' fatigue!

DRILL SEATED FORWARD GET-UPS

Aim
To develop multi-directional explosive acceleration; to improve a player's ability to get up and accelerate all in one movement.

Area/equipment
Indoor or outdoor area of 18 m².

Description
Player sits on the floor, facing in the direction he is going to run with legs straight out in front. On the coach's signal, the player gets up as quickly as possible, accelerates for 9 metres and then slows down before jogging gently back to the start position.

Key teaching points
- Try to complete the drill in one smooth action
- Use correct running form/mechanics (see pages 48–62)
- Do not stop between getting up and starting to run
- Get into an upright position and drive the arms as soon as possible
- Ensure that the initial steps are short and powerful
- Do not over-stride

Sets and reps
3 sets of 5 reps, with a jog-back recovery between each rep and a 2-minute recovery between each set.

Variations/progressions
- Seated backward get-ups
- Seated sideways get-ups
- Lying get-ups from the front, back, left and right sides
- Kneeling get-ups
- Work in pairs and have get-up competitions, with players chasing a ball
- Work in pairs with one player in front of the other; perform 'tag' get-ups

DRILL LET-GOES

Aim
To develop multi-directional explosive acceleration.

Area/equipment
Indoor or outdoor area of 18 m². Viper Belt with hand leash.

Description
Player 1 wears the Viper Belt and attempts to accelerate away in a straight line forwards while being resisted from behind by Player 2, who holds the hand leash to provide resistance. Player 2 maintains the resistance for a couple of seconds by shuffling and holding Player 1 as they slowly go forwards, before releasing Player 1, who explodes away. (If a Viper Belt and hand leash are not available, hold on to the shirt/top of Player 1.)

Key teaching points
- Player 1 should not lean or pull forwards excessively
- Use short steps during the explosion and acceleration phases
- Use a good arm drive
- Player 1 should adopt good running form/mechanics (see pages 48–62) as soon as possible after being released

Sets and reps
3 sets of 5 reps, with a walk-back recovery between each rep and a 2-minute recovery between each set.

Variations/progressions
- Lateral let-goes
- Backward let-goes
- Various angled let-goes
- Let-goes with an acceleration onto a drop ball, with the ball to be kicked before the second bounce

DRILL CHAIR GET-UPS

Aim
To develop explosive acceleration, linearly and laterally.

Area/equipment
Indoor or outdoor area of 18 m². Place a chair/stool and 5 Marker Spots as shown in figure 5.1.

Description
Player sits on the chair or portable box and, on the coach's signal, gets up and moves to the nominated marker as quickly as possible. On reaching the Marker Spot the player should decelerate and walk back to the start position. N.B. If a chair or box is not available the player may begin in a half squat position with arms reaching forward.

Key teaching points
■ Use an explosive arm drive when getting up
■ Get into a correct running posture as quickly as possible
■ Initial steps should be short and powerful
■ Work off the balls of the feet

Sets and reps
3 sets of 10 reps, with a walk-back recovery between each rep and a 2-minute recovery between each set.

Variations/progressions
■ Work in pairs; Player 1 stands 1 or 2 metres away from the chair with a ball in each hand and performs 'ball drops' by holding both arms out and dropping one of the balls for Player 2 (seated) to either trap or kick
■ Coach or player to stand behind the seated player and throw the ball over his shoulder. Seated player accelerates out of the chair to retrieve the ball

Figure 5.1 Chair get-ups

DRILL FLEXI-CORD – BUGGY RUNS

Aim
To develop multi-directional, explosive acceleration.

Area/equipment
Indoor or outdoor area with plenty of room for safe deceleration. Viper Belt with a flexi-cord attached at both ends by 2 anchor points. Place 3 Marker Spots in a line, 9 metres apart.

Description
Working in pairs, Player 1 wears the belt while Player 2 stands behind holding the flexi-cord, hands looped in and over the flexi-cord for safety purposes. Player 2 allows resistance to develop as Player 1 accelerates forwards, then runs behind maintaining constant resistance over the first 9 metres. Both players need to decelerate over the second 9 metres. Player 1 removes the belt after the required number of reps and completes a solo contrast run. The players then swap roles and repeat the drill.

Key teaching points
- Player 1 must focus on correct running form/mechanics (see pages 48–62) and explosive drive
- Player 2 works with Player 1, allowing the flexi-cord to provide the resistance
- Always perform the drill once without resistance immediately afterwards (contrast phase)

Sets and reps
1 set of 6 reps, plus 1 contrast run with a 30-second recovery between each rep and a 3-minute recovery before the next drill.

Variations/progressions
- Lateral buggy run – Player 1 accelerates laterally for the first 2 metres before turning to cover the remaining distance linearly
- After the acceleration phase of the contrast run, the coach can introduce a ball for the player to run on to

DRILL   *FLEXI-CORD – OUT AND BACK*

Aim
To develop short, explosive, angled accelerated runs.

Area/equipment
Large indoor or outdoor area of 9 m² (10 square yards) would be ideal. Viper Belt with a flexi-cord attached to 1 anchor point on the belt, and a safety belt on the other end of the flexi-cord. Marker Spots or cones set out as in Figure 5.2.

Description
Working in pairs, Player 1 wears the Viper Belt; Player 2 stands directly behind Player 1, holding the flexi-cord and wearing the safety belt. The flexi-cord should be taut at this stage. Player 2 nominates a Marker Spot for Player 1, alternating between the 3 Marker Spots for the required number of repetitions. Player 1 runs to the nominated marker, then returns to the start using short, sharp steps. Finish with a contrast run before swapping roles.

Key teaching points
- Focus on short, sharp, explosive steps and a fast, powerful arm drive
- Maintain correct running form/mechanics (see pages 48–62)
- Work off the balls of the feet
- Use short steps while returning back to the start, and keep bodyweight forwards

Sets and reps
3 sets of 6 reps plus 1 contrast run per set, with a 3-minute recovery between each set. For advanced players, depending on the time of the season, increase to 10 reps per set.

Variations/progressions
- Perform the drill laterally
- Perform the drill backwards

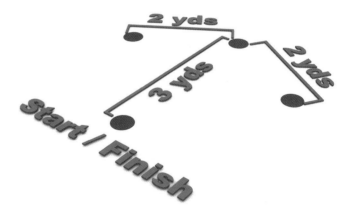

Figure 5.2 Flexi-cord – out and back

DRILL
FLEXI-CORD – LATERAL EXPLOSIVE
FIRST STEP DEVELOPMENT

Aim
To develop explosive lateral movement ability, particularly over the first few metres, with or without a ball at the feet.

Area/equipment
Indoor or outdoor area 11 m². Viper Belt or viper swivel belt; flexi-cord; balls; 13 Marker Spots set up as shown in figure 5.3(a).

Description
Player 1, wearing the Viper Belt, runs in a zigzag pattern between the markers. Player 2 works along the line between the 2 outside markers, slightly behind Player 1 to ensure that the flexi-cord does not get in the way of the arm mechanics. Work up and back along the line of markers. On completing the reps, Player 1 removes the belt and performs a contrast run.

Key teaching points
- Maintain correct running form/mechanics (see pages 48–62)
- Use short step when moving backwards
- Keep the hips square
- Player 2 should move along with Player 1, concentrating on maintaining the constant distance, angle and resistance
- No skipping
- Push off with the back foot – do not pull with the front foot

Sets and reps
3 sets of 6 reps (work both the left and right sides; just turn the belt around on the player's waist) plus 1 contrast run per set, with a 3-minute recovery between each set.

Variations/progressions
- Perform the drill backwards
- Perform the drill without the ball at a high intensity
- Replace the far side Marker Spots/cones with Spiked Poles or Mannequins. Player 1 to press to each Spiked Pole or Mannequin

Figure 5.3 Flexi-cord – lateral explosive first step development

DRILL FLEXI-CORD – VERTICAL POWER

Aim

To develop vertical take-off power for the production of more air time and height when jumping to head the ball, or to catch the ball as a goalkeeper.

Area/equipment

Indoor or outdoor area of approximately 3–4 m². 1 Viper Belt with 2 flexi-cords; 1 ball

Description

Working in groups of 4, 1 player wears the Viper Belt, which has 1 flexi-cord attached to each side by both of their ends (see photo). 2 players stand a yard away, one on either side of the resisted player. They stand on the flexi-cords with their legs about 1 metre apart. The fourth player stands in front of the resisted player, holding the ball above his head. The resisted player jumps to head the ball, goes back to the start position and repeats the drill.

Key teaching points

■ Maintain correct jumping form/mechanics for each rep (see page 42)
■ Do not sink in to the hips, either before take-off or on landing
■ Work off the balls of the feet
■ On landing, regain balance and prepare before the next jump

Sets and reps

3 sets of 8 reps plus 1 contrast jump, with a 3-minutes recovery between each set.

Variation/progression

Perform quick jumps – i.e. no setting between jumps. These are fast, repetitive jumps performed as quickly as possible.

DRILL FLEXI-CORD – OVERSPEED

Aim
To develop lightning-quick acceleration.

Area/equipment
Indoor or outdoor area. 1 Viper Belt with a flexi-cord attached. 4 Marker Spot/cones placed in a 'T' formation with 2 metres (2 yards) between each Marker Spot/cone.

Description
Working in pairs, Player 1 wears the Viper Belt and faces Player 2. Player 2 has the safety belt around his waist – i.e. the flexi-cord will go from belly button to belly button – and he holds the flexi-cord. Player 1 stands at Marker Spot/cone A. Player 2 stands at marker dot/cone B and walks backwards and away from Player 1, thereby increasing the resistance on the flexi-cord. After the flexi-cord has been stretched for 4–5 yards, Player 1 accelerates towards Player 2, who then nominates either Marker Spot/cone C or D, requiring Player 1 to explosively change direction. Both players walk back to the start and repeat the drill. See figure 5.4.

Key teaching points
- Maintain correct running form/mechanics (see pages 48–62)
- Control the running form/mechanics
- During the change of direction phase, shorten the steps and increase the rate of firing in the arms

Sets and reps
3 sets of 8 reps plus 1 contrast run, with a 3-minute recovery between each set.

Variations/progressions
- Player 1 starts with a horizontal jump before accelerating away
- Introduce a ball for Player 1 to run on to after the change of direction phase

Figure 5.4 Flexi-cord – overspeed

DRILL   *SIDE-STEPPER – LATERAL RUNS*

Aim
To develop explosive, controlled lateral running patterns.

Area/equipment
Indoor or outdoor area. 10–12 Marker Spots placed in a zigzag pattern and a Side-Stepper.

Description
Wearing the Side-Stepper, the player covers the length of the grid by running a lateral zigzag pattern between the Marker Spots. Just before arriving at each dot, he extends the last step to increase the level of resistance. On completing a run, he turns around and works back along the grid. See figure 5.5.

Key teaching points
■ Maintain correct lateral running form/mechanics (see pages 34–44)
■ Do not sink in to the hips when changing direction
■ During the change of direction phase, increase arm speed to provide additional control

Sets and reps
3 sets of 6 reps plus 1 contrast run, with no recovery time between each rep and a 3-minute recovery between each set.

Variations/progressions
■ Perform the drill backwards – i.e. using a jockeying movement
■ Include a ball

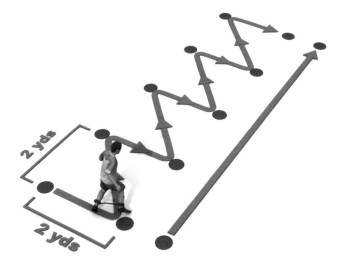

Figure 5.5 Side-Stepper – lateral runs

DRILL   SIDE-STEPPER – JOCKEYING IN PAIRS

Aim
To develop man-to-man marking skills, with a particular focus on defensive and attacking jockeying skills.

Area/equipment
Indoor or outdoor area. Side-Steppers. 6–8 Marker Spots. Mark out a channel approximately 18 metres (20 yards) long and 3 metres (3 yards) wide.

Description
Two players wearing Side-Steppers face each other approximately 2 metres apart. The attacking player moves from right to left in a jockeying pattern, while the defending player attempts to mirror the movements to prevent the attacking player from having too much space. In other words, the attacking player works in a forward direction and the defending player works backwards. See figure 5.6.

Key teaching points
- Use quick, low steps – not high knees
- No skipping or jumping – one foot should be in contact with the floor at all times
- Try to keep the feet shoulder-width apart
- Use a powerful arm drive
- Do not sink in to the hips

Sets and reps
3 sets of 4 reps plus a contrast set of 2 reps, with a 30-second recovery between each rep and a 2-minute recovery between each set.

Variations/progressions
- Both players perform the drill laterally, with one player leading and the other trying to mirror his movements
- Introduce a ball

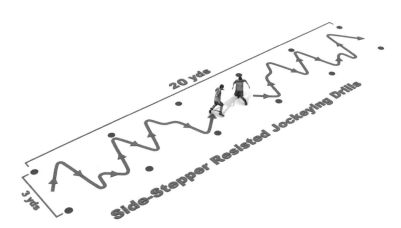

Figure 5.6 Side-Stepper – jockeying in pairs

DRILL   *HAND WEIGHT DROPS*

Aim
To develop explosive power, re-acceleration and, specifically, a powerful arm drive.

Area/equipment
Indoor or outdoor area. Light hand weights (1–2 kg in weight). Place 1 Marker Spot to represent the start, a second Marker Spot 14 metres (15 yards) away and a final Marker Spot 9 metres (10 yards) away from the second.

Description
Player holds the weights in his hands and accelerates to the second Marker Spot where he releases the hand weights and, keeping a natural flow to the arm mechanics, continues to accelerate to the third Marker Spot before decelerating and walking back to the start. Repeat the drill for the required number of reps. See figure 5.7.

Key teaching points
■ Maintain correct running form/mechanics (see pages 48–62)
■ Do not stop the arm drive to release the weights
■ Keep the head tall
■ Quality, not quantity, is vital

Sets and reps
3 sets of 4 reps, with a 3-minute recovery between each set.

Variations/progressions
■ On the release of the hand weights, the coach calls for a change of direction, i.e. the player has to accelerate off at different angles
■ Perform the drill backwards over the first 14 metres (15 yards), then turn, accelerate and release the weights to explode away
■ Perform the drill laterally over the first 14 metres (15 yards), then turn, accelerate and release the weights to explode away
■ On the release of the hand weights, a ball is thrown for the player to accelerate on to and control

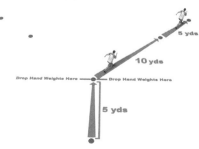

Figure 5.7 Hand weight drops

DRILL PARACHUTE RUNNING

Aim
To develop explosive running over longer distances (sprint endurance); to develop explosive re-acceleration.

Area/equipment
Indoor or outdoor area. 4 Marker Spots and a parachute. Mark out a grid 50 yards in length; place 1 Marker Spot for the start point and 3 further Marker Spots at distances of 30, 40 and 50 yards from the start marker.

Description
Wearing the parachute, the player accelerates to the 40-yard marker, then decelerates to the end of the grid.

Key teaching points
- Maintain correct running form/mechanics (see pages 48–62)
- Do not worry if the wind and the resistance make it feel as though you are being pulled from side to side; this will in fact improve your balance and co-ordination.
- Do not lean in to the run too much
- Quality, not quantity, is vital

Sets and reps
3 sets of 5 reps plus 1 contrast run, with a walk-back recovery between each rep and a 3-minute recovery between each set.

Variations/progressions
- Explosive re-acceleration using the parachute's release mechanism – the player accelerates to the 30-yard marker, where he releases the parachute, then explodes to the 40-yard Marker Spot before decelerating
- Random change of direction – the coach stands behind the 30-yard Marker Spot and, as the player releases the parachute, indicates a change in the direction of the run. When this has been mastered, the coach can introduce a ball for players to run on to during the explosive phase
- Add an additional parachute to increase resistance

DRILL BALL DROPS

Aim
To develop explosive reactions.

Area/equipment
Indoor or outdoor area. 1 or 2 balls.

Description
Working in pairs, Player 1 drops the ball from shoulder height at various distances and angles from his partner. Player 2 explodes forwards immediately and attempts to catch or trap the ball before the second bounce. Distances between players will differ because the height of the bounce will vary depending on the ground surface.

Key teaching points
- Work off the balls of the feet, particularly prior to the ball drop
- Use a very explosive arm drive
- The initial steps should be short, fast and explosive
- Do not jump, stutter or hesitate at the take-off
- Work on developing a smooth, one-movement run

Sets and reps
3 sets of 10 reps with a 2-minute recovery between each set.

Variations/progressions
- Player 1 to hold 2 balls and to drop just 1 in order that Player 2 has to anticipate and react
- Work in groups of 3, with 2 players at different angles alternately dropping a ball for the third player to catch or trap. On achieving this, the player turns and accelerates away to catch or trap the second ball
- Alter the start positions, e.g. sideways, backwards with a call, seated, etc.
- 2 players have to compete to be first to the ball

DRILL   SLED RUNNING

Aim
To develop explosive sprint endurance.

Area/equipment
Large outdoor grass area (preferable) and a Sprint Sled. Using Marker Spots, mark out an area 25–55 metres in length.

Description
Player is connected to the sled and sprints over the nominated distance before recovering, turning around and repeating the drill.

Key teaching points
- Maintain correct running form/mechanics (see pages 48–62)
- Maintain a strong arm drive
- Players will often need to use an exaggerated forward lean to initiate the momentum required to get the sled moving. As momentum picks up, the player should transfer into the correct running position

Sets and reps
2 sets of 5 reps plus 1 contrast run, with a 1-minute recovery between each rep and a 3-minute recovery between each set.

Variation/progressions
5-metre explosive acceleration – the player covers 45 metres by alternating between acceleration and deceleration phases over distances of 5 metres. N.B. Quality, not quantity, is the key here.

DRILL	W DRILL

Aim
To develop explosive angled forward and backward movements.

Area/equipment
Indoor or outdoor area. Viper Belt. Place 5 Marker Spots in a W formation, 5 metres (5 yards) wide at the top and 2 metres (2 yards) wide at the bottom, and 4 metres (4 yards) to its longest point and 2 metres to the centre point.

Description
Wearing the Viper Velt, Player 1 starts at point A of the W, moving under resistance backwards to point B, forwards to centre point C, backwards to point D and forwards to point E, which is 1 complete W. Player 2 works from behind and moves laterally to provide resistance as Player 1 moves across the W. See figure 5.8.

Key teaching points
- Focus on short, sharp, explosive steps
- Use a powerful arm drive
- Stay as tall as possible
- Do not sink into the hips
- Maintain correct running form at all times (see pages 48–62)
- Stay on the balls of the feet at all times
- Use short steps in resisted backward movements

Sets and reps
3 sets of 5 reps where 1 rep = 1 complete W, with a 2-minute recovery between each set.

Variations/progressions
- Perform the drill laterally
- Introduce a third player who stands in front of the W and passes a ball for Player 1 to return while performing the drill

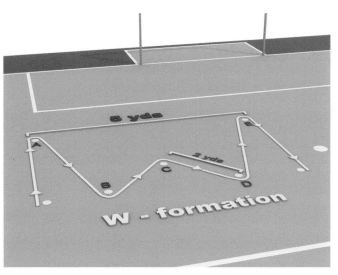

Figure 5.8 W drill

DRILL BREAK-AWAY MIRROR

Aim
To develop multi-directional explosive reactions.

Area/equipment
Indoor or outdoor area. Break-away Belt.

Description
Set a time limit. 2 players face each other attached by the break-away Belt. Player 1 is the proactive player while Player 2 is reactive. Player 1 attempts to get away from Player 2 by using sideways, forward or backward movements. Players are not allowed to turn around and run away. The drill ends if and when the proactive player breaks the belt connection, or the time runs out.

Key teaching points
■ Stay focused on your partner
■ Do not sink into the hips
■ Keep the head tall and the spine straight
■ Maintain correct arm mechanics (see pages 45–47)

Sets and reps
3 sets, where 1 set = 30 seconds of each player taking the proactive role, followed by a 1-minute recovery period.

Variations/progressions
■ Side-by-side mirror drills – the object is for the proactive player to move away laterally and gain as much distance as possible before the other can react
■ Players run through an agility circuit while connected by the break-away Belt

DRILL   *LATERAL SPEED DEVELOPMENT*

Aim
To develop explosive, controlled lateral ability; to develop precise and accurate control of the ball at speed under pressure.

Area/equipment
Indoor or outdoor area. Viper Belt with 2 flexi-cords (1 attached at each side); 2 short Fast Foot Ladders; balls; 2 Marker Spots.

Description
Player 1 is connected to Players 2 and 3 by the Viper Belt and 2 laterally fixed flexi-cords. Player 4 stands 5–10 metres away with the balls, in front of Player 1. The ladders are placed laterally on each side of Player 1, with a 1-metre gap in the centre. Players 2 and 3 stand on the Marker Spots at either end of the ladders, providing resistance from both sides. The drill commences with Player 4 passing a ball to either side of Player 1, who moves laterally down the ladder under resistance from one side to return the ball. The drill continues in this manner for the required number of reps. When the reps have been completed the drill is performed without resistance (contrast phase).

Key teaching points
- Reassert good arm mechanics when possible
- Maintain correct running form/mechanics (see pages 48–62)
- Use short, explosive steps

Sets and reps
3 sets of 8 reps plus 2 contrast runs, with a 3-minute recovery between each set.

Variations/progressions
- Perform the drill without the ladders
- Work in a sand pit or use high jump landing mats so Player 1 can lunge and dive to return the ball
- Player 1 to wear a Side-Stepper; this will increase the resistance on the legs
- Loosen the Viper Belt so that Player 1 can turn inside the belt. Position players on each side to pass the ball, requiring Player 1 to turn and return the ball

Figure 5.10 Lateral speed development

DRILL MEDICINE BALL (JELLY BALL) WORKOUT

Aim
To develop explosive upper-body and core power.

Area/equipment
Indoor or outdoor area. Medicine balls (Jelly Balls) of various weights.

Description
Working in pairs or against a solid wall, players perform simple throws, e.g. chest passes, single-arm passes, front slams, back slams, twist passes, woodchoppers and granny throws.

Key teaching points
- Start with a lighter ball for a warm-up set
- Start with simple movements before progressing to twists etc.
- Keep the spine upright
- Take care when loading (catching) and unloading (throwing) as this can put stress on the lower back.

Sets and reps
1 set of 12 reps of each drill with a 1-minute recovery between each drill and a 3-minute recovery before the next exercise.

Variations/progressions
- Front slam
- Back slam
- Woodchopper
- Chest pass
- Single-arm thrust
- Side slam
- Backward throw
- Throw-in

Front slam

Back slam

Woodchopper

MEDICINE BALL (JELLY BALL) WORKOUT (Contd...)

Chest pass

Backward throw

Single-arm thrust

Throw-in

Side slam

DRILL ASSISTED RESISTED TOW RUNS

Aim
To develop explosive running.

Area/equipment
Large indoor or outdoor area. Viper Belt.

Description
Players 1 and 2 are attached to each other by the Viper Belt. Player 1 runs away from Player 2, who stands still until the resistance is strong, then is pulled forwards. This acceleration is assisted. Player 1 now decelerates until he feels the resistance from behind diminish, then accelerates again under resistance. The process is repeated for the length of the space available.

Key teaching points
- Maintain correct running form/mechanics (see pages 48–62)
- Both players should use a strong arm drive
- Both players should use short steps during the acceleration and deceleration phases

Sets and reps
2 sets of 6 reps with a 30-second recovery between each rep and a 2-minute recovery between each set.

Variation/Progression
Vary the starting position.

DRILL

PLYOMETRICS –
LOW-IMPACT QUICK JUMPS

Aim

To develop explosive power for running, jumping and changing direction.

Area/equipment

Indoor or outdoor area. Fast Foot Ladder or Marker Spots placed at 18-inch intervals.

Description

The player performs double-footed single jumps, i.e. 1 jump between each rung or Marker Spot. On reaching the end he turns around and jumps back. See figure 5.9(a).

Key teaching points

■ Maintain correct jumping form/mechanics (see page 42)
■ The emphasis is on the speed of the jumps, not the height
■ Start slowly and increase the speed gradually, but do not lose control – avoid feeling as though you are going to 'fall over the edge of a cliff' when you reach the end of the drill
■ Do not lean forwards too much

Figure 5.9(a) Plyometrics – low-impact quick jumps

Sets and reps

2 sets of 2 reps with a 1-minute recovery between each set.

Variations/progressions

■ Backwards jumps.
■ Perform 2 jumps forwards followed by 1 jump back – see figure 5.9 (b)
■ Sideways jumps
■ Sideways jumps, 2 forwards and 1 back
■ Hopscotch – 2 feet in 1 square and then 1 foot either side of the next square
■ Left- and right-footed hops
■ Increase the intensity – replace the Fast Foot Ladders or Marker Spots with 18- or 30-cm hurdles

Figure 5.9(b) Plyometics – low-impact quick jumps – 2 forwards and 1 back

DRILL PLYOMETRICS – PLYOMETRIC CIRCUIT

Aim
To develop explosive multi-directional speed, agility and quickness.

Area/equipment
Indoor or outdoor area. Place Fast Foot Ladders, hurdles (Micro and Macro) and Marker Spots in a circuit formation. See figure 5.10.

Description
Players jump, hop and zigzag their way through the circuit as stipulated by the coach.

Key teaching points
■ Maintain the correct mechanics for each part of the circuit (see pages 34–44)
■ Ensure that there is a smooth transfer from running to jumping movements and vice versa

Sets and reps
5 circuits with a 1-minute recovery between each circuit.

Variations/progressions
Work in pairs. Player 1 completes the circuit while Player 2 feeds him the ball at various points around the circuit (i.e. to head, chest or kick as necessary).

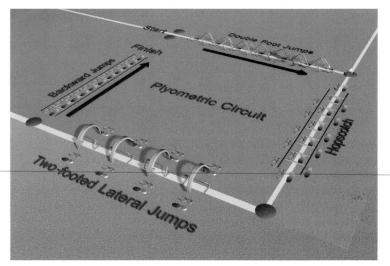

Figure 5.10 Plyometrics – plyometric circuit

DRILL   *PLYOMETRICS – DROP JUMPS*

Aim
To develop explosive multi-directional speed.

Area/equipment
Indoor or outdoor area with a cushioned or grassed landing surface. A stable platform or bench to jump from of variable height – 40–90 cm, depending on the stage in the season.

Description
Player stands on the platform and jumps off with his feet together, lands on the balls of the feet and then accelerates away for 5 metres.

Key teaching points
- Do not land flat-footed
- Do not sink into the hips on landing
- Maintain a strong core
- Keep the head up – this will help to align the spine

Sets and reps
2 sets of 10 reps, with a 3-minute recovery between each set.

Variations/progressions
- Backward drop jumps, turning through 180 degrees before sprinting off
- Side drop jumps, turning and sprinting off
- Introduce a ball for the players to accelerate on to

CHAPTER 6 EXPRESSION OF POTENTIAL

SHORT COMPETITIVE TEAM GAMES THAT PREPARE PLAYERS FOR THE NEXT LEVEL OF TRAINING

This stage is quite short in duration, but very important, as it brings together all the elements of the SAQ Continuum into highly competitive, and even enjoyable, situations involving other players.

Short, high-intensity 'tag' type games and random agility tests work really well here. The goal is to place players and their newly practised movement skills under competitive pressure. This gives the coach the opportunity to assess the players' performance and see whether they can cope with the pressure or if they revert to bad habits.

The key is to fire up your players and get them to perform fast, explosive, controlled and random movements that leave them exhilarated and mentally and physically ready for the next stage of training or the next game.

DRILL   BRITISH BULLDOG

Aim
To practise multi-directional, explosive movements in a pressured situation.

Area/equipment
Indoor or outdoor area of approximately 18 m². 20 Marker Spots to mark out starting and finishing lines.

Description
One player is nominated and stands in the centre of the grid, while the rest stand at one side behind the start line. On the coach's call, all of the players attempt to get to the opposite side of the square without being caught by the player in the middle. When the player in the middle captures another player, he joins them in the middle and helps capture more 'prisoners'. See figure 6.1.

Key teaching points
- Use correct mechanics at all times (see pages 34–44)
- Keep the head and eyes up to avoid collisions with other players

Sets and reps
Play for approximately 3–4 minutes before moving on to the more technical aspects of the game.

Variations/progressions
The player in the middle uses a ball to touch other players in order to capture them. The ball may be either kicked or thrown.

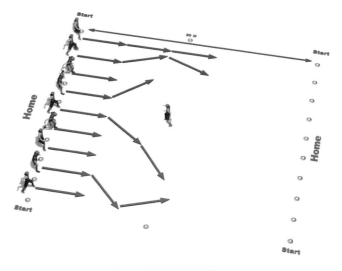

Figure 6.1 British Bulldog

DRILL   *CIRCLE BALL*

Aim
To practise using explosive evasion skills.

Area/equipment
Indoor or outdoor area. Balls. Players make a circle about 14 metres in diameter (depending on the size of the squad).

Description
1 or 2 players stand in the centre of the circle while the players on the outside have 1 or 2 balls between them. The object is for those on the outside to try to make contact (with the ball) with those on the inside. The players on the inside try to avoid or dodge the balls. The winners are the pair with the least number of hits during their time in the centre. See figure 6.2.

Key teaching point
The players on the inside should use the correct mechanics (see pages 34–44).

Sets and reps
Each pair to stay in the centre area for 45 seconds.

Variation/progression
Players in the middle have to hold on to each other's hand or use a break-away Belt.

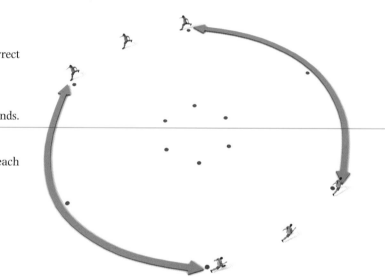

Figure 6.2 Circle ball

DRILL ROBBING THE NEST

Aim
To practise multi-directional explosive speed, agility and quickness.

Area/equipment
Indoor or outdoor area. Using Marker Spots, mark out a large outer circle about 22 metres in diameter and an inner circle measuring 2 metres in diameter. Place a number of balls in the inner circle.

Description
2 nominated players defend the 'nest' of balls with the rest of the players standing outside the outer circle (the 'safe zone'). The game starts when the outside players run in and try to steal the balls from the nest, by dribbling to the safe zone. The 2 defenders try to prevent the robbers from getting the balls to the safe zone by tagging them or getting in their way. For every successful tag and prevention, the ball is returned to the centre circle. See figure 6.3.

Key teaching points
■ Correct mechanics must be used at all times (see pages 34–44)
■ Players should dodge, swerve, weave, side-step, etc.
■ Light contact only should be used

Sets and reps
Each pair to defend for about 45 seconds.

Variation/progression
Defenders work together either by holding hands or interlocking arms; they will have to work hard to prevent the robbers.

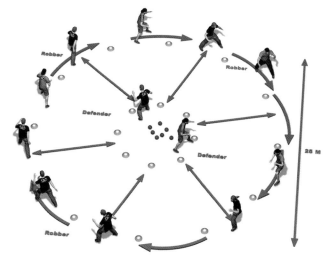

Figure 6.3 Robbing the nest

DRILL | *ODD ONE OUT*

Aim
To practise speed, agility and quickness in a competitive environment.

Area/equipment
Indoor or outdoor area. Marker Spots; balls. Mark out an outer circle 25 metres in diameter and an inner circle about 2 metres in diameter.

Description
Place a number of balls in the centre area, 1 fewer than the number of players present. The players are situated on the outside of the outer circle. On the coach's call, they start running around the outer circle; on the coach's second call, they collect a ball from the inner circle as quickly as possible. The player without a ball is out and performs a ball-skill drill as directed by the coach. The coach then removes another ball and repeats the process until there is only one player left. See figure 6.4.

Key teaching points
- Correct mechanics must be used at all times (see pages 34–44)
- Players should be aware of the other players around them

Sets and reps
Play the game until a winner emerges.

Variation/Progression
Work in pairs, joined together by holding hands or using a break-away Belt, with 1 ball between 2 players. If a pair break away from each other, they are disqualified.

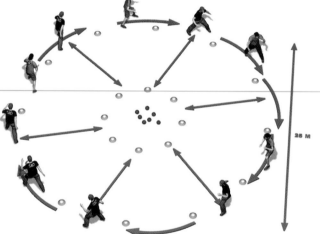

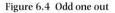

Figure 6.4 Odd one out

DRILL MARKER TURNS

Aim
To practise multi-directional speed, agility and quickness.

Area/equipment
Indoor or outdoor area of about 18 m² and 50 Marker Spots. Place the Marker Spots in and around the grid; 25 of them should be turned upside down.

Description
Working in two small teams (2–3 players per team), one team attempts to turn over the upright markers and the other team attempts to turn over the upside-down markers. The winner is the team with the largest number of markers their way around after 60 seconds. See figure 6.5.

Key teaching points
■ Initiate good arm drive after turning a marker
■ Use correct multi-directional mechanics
■ Be aware of other players around the area

Sets and reps
A game should last for 60 seconds.

Variation/progression
Use 4 teams and 4 different-coloured markers.

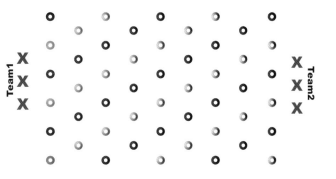

Figure 6.5 Marker turns

CHAPTER 7 VISION AND REACTION

DEVELOPING VISUAL ABILITY FOR FOOTBALL

Many players involved in football who have 20/20 vision assume that their visual ability for the sport will be competent. However, most eye tests only provide results for static visual acuity, that is a person's ability to identify certain letters on an eye chart. In contrast, football players use a whole range of visual abilities whenever decisions need to be made and movements into areas need to be completed, particularly when getting into position to cut off a pass, tracking the ball in the air and visually assessing the opposition's movements and position.

The drills in this chapter will help to develop:

■ dynamic visual acuity – the ability to maintain the clarity of an object while moving

■ colour vision – the ability to recognise the various colours of the spectrum

■ depth perception – the ability to judge distances rapidly and accurately

■ visual reaction time – the time required to perceive and respond to visual stimulation

■ central-peripheral awareness – the ability to pay attention to what you are looking at, yet to be aware of what is going on around you without moving your eyes and losing the central focus

■ eye–hand–body co-ordination – the ability to integrate the eyes, hands and body as a whole unit

Simple yet scientifically complex equipment is used in this section, including Visual Acuity Rings, Peripheral Vision Sticks and Visual Enhancement Training Goggles.

DRILL   *VISUAL ACUITY*
EYE–HAND REACTION DEVELOPMENT

Aim
To develop fast, accurate visual skills including colour vision and visual reaction time.

Area/equipment
Indoor or outdoor area. Visual Acuity Ring.

Description
Working in pairs, Player 1 throws the ring so that it rotates in the air to Player 2. Prior to throwing, Player 1 nominates one of the coloured balls attached to the ring for Player 2 to visually track and catch. Gradually increase the speed of the spin on the visual acuity ring as proficiency improves. See figure 7.1.

Key teaching points
■ Keep the head still – move the eyes to track the ring
■ Work off the balls of the feet at all times
■ The hands should be out and in front of the body, ready to catch the ring

Sets and reps
2 sets of 20 reps with a 1-minute recovery between each set.

Variations/progressions
■ Turn and catch
■ Throw the ring sideways
■ Instead of catching the ball on the ring, kick or head the ball

Figure 7.1 Visual acuity eye–hand reaction development

DRILL PERIPHERAL AWARENESS

Aim
To develop peripheral awareness; to help players detect and react to the ball coming from behind and from the side more quickly.

Area/equipment
Indoor or outdoor area. Peripheral Vision Stick.

Description
Work in pairs with Player 1 behind Player 2, who stands in a ready position. Player 1 holds the stick and moves it from behind Player 2 into his field of vision. As soon as Player 2 detects the stick, he claps both hands over the ball at the end of the stick or glances the ball with the head. See figure 7.2.

Key teaching points
■ Player 2 should work off the balls of the feet and in a slightly crouched position with the hands held out ready (an athletic position)
■ Player 1 must be careful not to touch any part of Player 2's body with the stick
■ Player 1 should vary the speed at which the stick is brought into Player 2's field of vision

Sets and reps
2 sets of 20 reps with no recovery between each rep and a 1-minute recovery between each set.

Variations/progressions
■ Instead of using a Peripheral Vision Stick, throw balls from behind Player 2 for him to fend off
■ Use 2 Peripheral Vision Sticks; as one is brought into Player 2's vision, use the other stick on the other side. Player 2 has to respond quickly with two movements

Figure 7.2 Peripheral vision

DRILL   REACTION BALL

Aim
To develop lightning-quick reactions.

Area/equipment
Indoor or outdoor area, but not a grass surface. 1 Reaction Ball or a rugby ball.

Description
Work in pairs, standing 5 metres apart. Player 1 throws the ball so that it bounces in front of Player 2; because of the structure of the ball it will bounce in any direction. Player 2 has to react and catch the ball before it bounces for a second time. See figure 7.3.

Key teaching points
- The player catching the ball should work off the balls of the feet and in a slightly crouched position with the hands out ready
- The ball should not be thrown hard – it will do the necessary work itself

Sets and reps
2 sets of 20 reps with no recovery between each rep and a 1-minute recovery between each set.

Variations/progressions
- Work individually or in pairs by throwing the ball against the wall
- Stand on agility discs while throwing the ball to each other
- Players to either kick or control the ball with the feet and the body

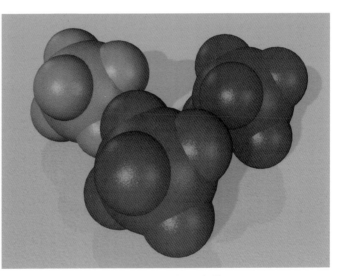

Figure 7.3 Reaction ball

DRILL FOLLOW THE THUMB

Aim
To develop all-round and peripheral vision.

Area/equipment
Indoor or outdoor area.

Description
Hold either arm out in front and make the 'thumbs up' sign. Keeping the head still and only moving the eyes, move the thumb up, down and around, following it with the eyes, moving to the extremes of the range of vision. Start slowly and gradually increase the speed of the movement.

Key teaching points
- Sit or stand upright with good posture
- Try the drill with both hands
- Keep the head still – do not move it
- Move only the eyes

Sets and reps
5 sets of 1-minute reps with a 30-second recovery between each set.

Variations/progressions
- While performing the drill, get another player to throw a ball to return and control (once in each set)
- Perform the drill while standing on an Agility Disc

DRILL *TRACKING AND FOCUS*

Aim
To develop ball-tracking ability and to make subtle focus adjustments.

Area/equipment
Indoor or outdoor area. Balls.

Description
Draw numbers or letters on 4 sides of the ball – use black ink on white/yellow balls, with the lettering no more than $1^1/_2$ inches in height. 2 players stand 14–18 metres apart. Player 1 holds up the ball for 2 seconds so that a number is clearly facing Player 2. Player 2 calls out the number as the ball is passed, and then returns the ball. The drill is now reversed. See figure 7.4.

Key teaching points
■ Keep the head still
■ Move the eyes, not the head

Sets and reps
5 sets of 12 reps with a 30-second recovery between each set.

Variations/progressions
■ Vary the time for which the ball is held up
■ Vary the distance between the players
■ Vary the angle from which the ball is passed

Figure 7.4 Tracking and focus

DRILL   DYNAMIC VISUAL ACUITY TRAINING

Aim
To develop ball-tracking skills while in motion; this drill also assists the ability to focus on an opponent while he is in action.

Area/equipment
Indoor or outdoor area. 8 balls.

Description
Number the balls 1–8, ensuring that ball 1 has the figure 1 marked on 6 sides of the ball and so on. Use black ink on white/yellow balls. 2 players stand 14–18 metres apart. Player 1 holds up a ball so that Player 2 cannot see what number is on it, then passes it towards Player 2, who calls out what number ball has been passed while it is in the air or on the ground, before controlling and passing the ball back. Player 1 passes the balls to Player 2 in a random order. See figure 7.5.

Key teaching points
- Keep the head still
- Move the eyes, not the head
- Maintain an athletic position
- Work on the balls of the feet

Sets and reps
5 sets of 12 reps with a 30-second recovery between each set.

Variations/progressions
- Vary the distance between the players
- Vary the angle at which the ball is passed
- Each player has 4 balls and pairs alternate the call between them
- Goalkeepers should catch the ball

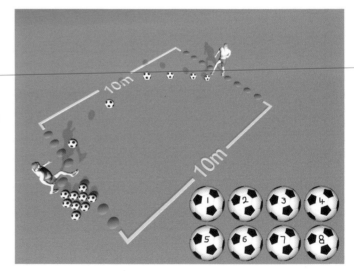

Figure 7.5 Dynamic visual acuity training

DRILL   BALL PLACEMENT DECISION-MAKING

Aim
To develop quick ball placement decision-making.

Area/equipment
Indoor or outdoor area. Bag of different-coloured balls.

Description
Use a bag of 3 different-coloured balls, i.e. yellow, orange, white (balls can be partly coloured with an indelible ink pen). The two players decide which colour ball represents which side a 1–2 will be played, e.g. the white ball means it will be played to the left-hand side of the receiving player, orange means in the middle and yellow to the right. The drill commences with Player 1 passing one of the balls to Player 2, who then plays the 1–2 on the agreed side of the pitch. The roles are then reversed. See figure 7.6

Key teaching points
■ Keep the head still; move the eyes only
■ Maintain an athletic position
■ Ensure that the ball is delivered quickly, forcing the receiving player to identify the colour of the ball while it is in the air

Sets and reps
1 bag of balls per player equals one set.

Variations/progressions
■ Vary the distance between the players
■ Vary the angle at which the ball is served
■ Vary the type of pass
■ Hide the balls behind the ball bag so that the receiving player can only see the colour of the ball once it has been delivered
■ Goalkeepers to catch the ball and then kick or throw it to an agreed area of the pitch

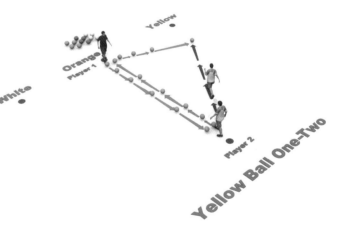

Figure 7.6 Ball placement decision-making

DRILL   *VISUAL ENHANCEMENT TRAINING (VET)*

Aim
To improve the ability of the eyes to focus and track and make subtle focus adjustments and alignments.

Area/equipment
Indoor or outdoor area. Visual Enhancement Training Goggles. Balls.

Description
Player 1 (outfield player or goalkeeper) wears the VET goggles. Player 2 stands at different angles and distances from Player 1 and proceeds to pass the ball from different angles and heights to Player 1, who controls and returns the ball. This continues for at least 10 minutes. The goggles are then removed and the drill is continued for another 2–3 minutes. The drill is now reversed.

Key teaching points
■ Maintain focus and track the ball at all times
■ Maintain an athletic position

Sets and reps
1 set equals 10 minutes with goggles and 2–3 minutes without. Perform 2 sets each with a 1-minute recovery between sets.

Variation/progression
Use more than one pair of goggles and perform group combination skills.

CHAPTER 8

BALANCE, CO-ORDINATION, FEEL AND JUDGEMENT

THE DEVELOPMENT OF BALANCE, CO-ORDINATION AND BODY AWARENESS

Other important physical attributes required by football players include the ability to be balanced and well co-ordinated in all movements, and the physical and spatial awareness (feel) necessary to transfer power in a game that places ever-changing demands on the individual. During a counter-attack, a player explodes into space, then stops in an instant with tremendous balance and co-ordination to lose a defensive marker. He then receives the ball and, with a deft touch, control, power and grace, flicks the ball past another defender with perfect timing so that a fellow forward can run on to the ball and place it wide of the goalkeeper into the back of the net. All of these skills can be trained and developed over a period of time.

DRILL FEEL AND DISTANCE

Aim
To develop feel and judgement of distance while manipulating balls of different weights and sizes.

Area/equipment
Indoor or outdoor area. 4 bins or small pop-up nets; Marker Spots/cones; assorted balls of different sizes, different weights and different materials (e.g. leather, plastic, foam).

Description
4 bins are placed in a line 5 metres apart with the balls placed around a Marker Spot a further 5 metres from the first bin. Player picks out any ball and attempts to kick the ball into one of the bins, then selects a different ball and attempts to kick it into the same bin as the first ball. This is continued until all the balls have been used. The drill recommences with the player collecting the balls and repeating the drill, this time aiming at a different bin. See figure 8.1.

Key teaching points
- Stand in an athletic position
- Keep the head still

Sets and reps
Perform the drill until all the balls have been used.

Variations/progressions
- During the set, vary from bin to bin
- Work in pairs; players to pass the ball between them and then target a bin
- Goalkeepers can throw or roll the ball into the bins

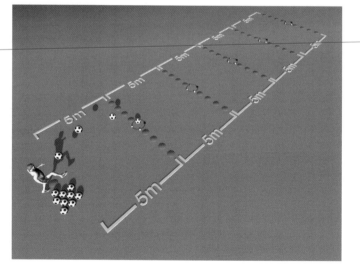

Figure 8.1 Feel and distance

DRILL   *LILY PAD DRILL*

Aim
To develop dynamic balance, co-ordination and proprioception.

Area/equipment
Indoor or outdoor area. 8 Agility Discs; Balls.

Description
Place the Agility Discs so that players can walk from one to another. Player 1 stands 4 or 5 yards away. Player 2 starts the drill by walking down the row of Agility Discs; Player 1 passes or throws the ball for Player 2 to control with either foot or the head or chest and volley back while balancing on the disc. See figure 8.2.

Key teaching points
- Start in an athletic position
- Maintain a strong core
- Look up and focus on the ball, not on the agility discs
- Do not sink into the hips

Sets and reps
1 set equals 3 reps. Perform 3 sets with a 30-second recovery between sets.

Variations/progressions
- Perform the drill laterally
- Increase the distance between the Agility Discs, therefore changing the players' stance

Figure 8.2 Lily pad drill

DRILL BALANCE BEAM WALK

Aim

To develop proprioception, balance and co-ordination.

Area/equipment

Indoor or outdoor area. Balls; balance beam.

Description

Player 1 stands 4 or 5 metres away. Player 2 commences the drill by standing on the balance beam and gradually walking down its length. Player 1 passes or throws the ball to Player 2, who passes it back without losing his balance. This is continued for the length of the balance beam. See figure 8.3.

Key teaching points

- Start in an athletic position
- Maintain a strong core
- Look up and focus on the ball, not the balance beam
- Do not sink into the hips

Sets and reps

1 set equals 3 reps. Perform 3 sets with a 30-second recovery between sets.

Variations/progressions

- Perform the drill laterally
- Goalkeepers to catch and throw the ball back
- When perfected, players can control the ball in the air for 2–3 touches and then return it

Figure 8.3 Balance beam walk

DRILL   MINI-TRAMPOLINE MANIPULATIONS

Aim
To develop proprioception, balance, co-ordination and manipulation skills.

Area/equipment
Indoor or outdoor area. Balls; mini-trampoline.

Description
Player stands on the mini-trampoline and gradually starts to rebound while performing keepy-up with the ball. The player should increase his speed as confidence and skills improve.

Key teaching points
- Start in an athletic position
- Maintain a strong core
- Do not sink into the hips

Sets and reps
3 sets of 2 minutes, with a 30-second recovery between sets.

Variation/progression
Work in pairs. Player 1 rebounds while Player 2 delivers the ball for Player 1 to return.

CHAPTER 9

POSITION–SPECIFIC PATTERNS OF MOVEMENT

THE DEVELOPMENT OF MULTI-DIRECTIONAL AND EXPLOSIVE SPEED IN A FOOTBALL-SPECIFIC CONTEXT INCLUDING RESISTED, ASSISTED, OVERSPEED, VERTICAL AND HORIZONTAL POWER DEVELOPMENT TECHNIQUES

In this section examples of position-specific patterns of movement are provided. By combining all areas of the SAQ Continuum – including techniques, equipment and drills – into game- and position-specific situations, you can improve and perfect players' movement skills.

The primary aim is to improve the explosive speed, precision, control, power and co-ordination necessary for specific movements required by each position in all areas of the field. These are best introduced when the foundation work of SAQ has been mastered and during training sessions that focus on the positional techniques of individual players.

| DRILL | WING BACK – ATTACKING WING BACK DRILL |

Aim

To develop acceleration and speed of attack on the flanks, and control of deceleration; to develop the control and agility required to jockey backwards, turn and accelerate back to defend.

Area/equipment

For maximum impact the drill should be performed in the relevant position on the pitch. 3 Fast Foot Ladders, balls and Marker Spots arranged as shown in figure 9.1.

Drill

The wing back accelerates down the first ladder and passes the ball at the end infield to a waiting player or coach. The wing back then accelerates over 28 metres (30 yards) to the start of the next ladder, where he decelerates as he works his way up. On leaving the second ladder, he crosses the ball at the end into the opposition's box. He then jockeys backwards for 9 metres (10 yards) (between the Marker Spots), keeping an eye on the result of the crossed ball, before turning and accelerating through the third ladder and sprinting back to the start Marker Spot.

Key teaching points

- Concentrate on correct mechanics in all phases of sprinting, including acceleration and deceleration (see pages 34–44)
- Concentrate on the turn; this needs to be perfected as poor turns can cost 2–3 metres
- Ensure correct techniques are used when the player is on the ball
- Work on both the left and right sides of the pitch

Sets and reps

6 reps, with a 2-minute recovery between each rep.

Variations/progressions

- Work in pairs with 1 player feeding the ball in at various stages throughout the drill
- Place marker dots in the 28-metre sprint area for swerves and zigzags

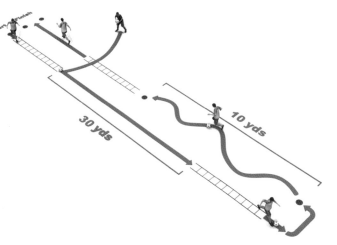

Figure 9.1 Wing back – attacking wing back drill

DRILL — ALL DEFENDERS – PASSING A CLEARED BALL

Aim
To develop the ability to defend the ball when it has been cleared from a dangerous position, e.g. crosses, set pieces and shots that require getting the ball away quickly; to develop an understanding of the need to press and close down the space between players and the ball.

Area/equipment
For maximum impact the drill should be performed in the relevant position on the pitch. Light hand weights and 8 Marker Spots/cones marking out a grid as shown in figure 9.2.

Description
The defender starts in a position between Marker Spots/cones A and B, holding the hand weights. On the coach's call, the player moves forwards and backwards between the 2 Marker Spots/cones. The coach then nominates 1 of the 6 outfield Marker Spots/cones to represent where the ball has been cleared to. The player turns, accelerates and, after the first 4–5 steps, drops the weights and explodes to the Marker Spot/cone. On completion of the drill the player jogs back to the starting position.

Key teaching points
- Maintain correct running form/mechanics (see pages 48–62)
- Use short steps and a strong arm drive when turning and accelerating
- Hand weights to be dropped as part of the running technique: do not stop or allow the arm mechanics to falter

Sets and reps
3 sets of 5 reps plus 1 contrast run with a 2-minute recovery between each set.

Variations/progressions
- Introduce jumping as if for a ball prior to the acceleration phase
- Remove the outfield Marker Spots/cones and replace them with players. Each player has a ball and the defender presses the nominated player who takes the defender on

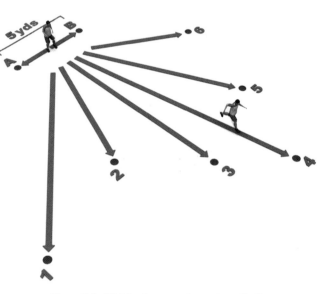

Figure 9.2 All defenders – passing a cleared ball

DRILL
ALL DEFENDERS –
CUTTING ACROSS YOUR OPPONENT

Aim
A primary concern for a defender in front of goal is to get in front of and across the attacking opponent, cutting off their ball supply; this drill develops this skill with controlled explosion.

Area/equipment
For maximum impact the drill should be performed in the relevant position on the pitch. Ball, Marker Spots/cones and a Viper Belt with 2 flexi-cords attached, 1 to each side. Set the Marker Spots/cones out as shown in figure 9.3(a).

Description
Work in groups of 4, with Player 1 wearing the Viper Belt. Player 2 holds a flexi-cord and stands directly behind Player 1. Player 3 holds the other flexi-cord and stands to either the left or right of Player 1. Player 4 stands further down the grid, ready to deliver a ball. Player 1 accelerates down the grid; Player 2 stands still and provides resistance; and Player 3 runs laterally in line with Player 1. When Player 1 reaches the area between markers A and B, he side-steps towards marker D. Meanwhile, Player 3 stands still at marker C to provide a lateral resistance. On reaching marker D, Player 1 receives a ball delivered by player 4 that he heads, chests or side-foots back. Player 1 then jockeys back to the starting position. See figure 9.3(b).

Figure 9.3(a) All defenders – cutting across
your opponent – setup

Key teaching points
- Maintain correct running form/mechanics (see pages 48–62)
- When moving laterally, ensure that players do not skip, sink into the hips or allow their feet to cross
- Encourage players to use small steps when moving laterally

Sets and reps
2 sets of 8 reps (4 moving to the left and 4 moving to the right) plus 1 contrast run with a 2-minute recovery between each set.

Figure 9.3(b) All defenders – cutting across your opponent

DRILL MIDFIELDERS – PALMER DRILL

Aim

To develop speed, agility and control in a progressive centre-field pressing drill – the object is to cut off attacking moves through the heart of the defence.

Area/equipment

For maximum impact the drill should be performed in the relevant position on the pitch. 2 Fast Foot Ladders and Marker Spots/cones placed in the formation shown in figure 9.4.

Description

The player accelerates down the ladder and moves explosively at the appropriate angle to the Marker Spot/cone nominated by the coach. Having reached the nominated Marker Spot/cone, the player jockeys backwards to the start/finish line.

Key teaching points

- Maintain correct running form/mechanics (see pages 48–62)
- Develop awareness by looking up while moving through the ladders
- Maintain an explosive arm drive during the change of direction phase
- Ensure that players work both to the left and right of the ladder

Sets and reps

1 set of 8 reps (coach should try to call 4 to the left and 4 to the right) with 15-second recovery intervals between reps.

Variation/progression

This variation involves the second ladder. The aim is to develop the centre-half's explosive speed, and to close down an attacker who has decelerated early to draw the centre-half out of defence – timing is crucial. The centre-half accelerates down the first ladder, then sprints to the second ladder and decelerates down this one. On leaving the second ladder, the player moves explosively at the appropriate angle to the nominated Marker Spot/cone, jockeys backwards for a few yards, turns and accelerates back to the start/finish line.

Figure 9.4 Midfielders – Palmer drill

DRILL | MIDFIELDERS –
BACKWARD TURN AND COVER

Aim

Teams may tactically attempt to bypass midfield players by using the ball over the top. This requires the defensive midfielder to anticipate the direction of the pass by keeping an eye on the ball while covering backwards. When the pass is delivered, the player is required to turn, accelerate and cover. The speed of the turn and acceleration to cover is crucial, and is developed with this drill.

Area/equipment

For maximum impact the drill should be performed in the relevant position on the pitch. 12 Marker Spots/cones and a Viper Belt with a leash attachment (if you do not have a Viper Belt and leash, you can use a towel around the player's waist). Place the Marker Spots/cones in a fan formation with the outer Marker Spots/cones representing the numbers on a clock face. See figure 9.5.

Description

Work in pairs, with Player 1 wearing the Viper Belt and Player 2 providing resistance by holding the leash attachment. Player 1 faces Player 2 and moves backwards to a nominated inner Marker Spot/cone. Player 2 provides some resistance but does move with Player 1. On arriving at the Marker Spot/cone, Player 1 is released by Player 2 letting go of the leash. Player 1 explodes into a turn and sprints to a nominated outer Marker Spot/cone.

Key teaching points

- Maintain an upright position while moving backwards
- Use a strong arm drive while moving backwards
- On the turn, keep the feet shoulder-width apart – do not allow the feet to cross over
- After the turn, as the player comes into the linear position, encourage him to adopt an upright sprinting posture as soon as possible
- Player 2 should use short steps

Sets and reps

1 set of 6 reps, with a walk-back recovery between each rep and a 3-minute recovery before starting the next exercise.

Variations/progressions

- On Player 1's release, the coach delivers a ball to an outer marker. The player must explode to the ball and retrieve it
- A player with the ball moves between the outside Marker Spots/cones. On the coach's call, Player 1 turns, explodes and initiates a tackle on the player with the ball, whose aim is to beat Player 1

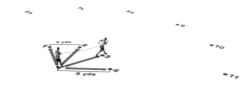

Figure 9.5 Midfielders – backward turn and cover

| DRILL | *ATTACKING MIDFIELDERS –*
TURN AND ATTACK |

Aim

To develop explosive, precise turn-and-chase skills. Midfielders often face their own goal, waiting for the ball to be cleared by the defender or the goalkeeper. On many occasions the ball will go over the midfielder, who will turn explosively, chase and regain the ball before setting up an attacking opportunity.

Area/equipment

For maximum impact the drill should be performed in the relevant position on the pitch. Light hand weights and Marker Spots/cones set up in a 'Y' formation as shown in figure 9.6.

Description

Holding the hand weights, the player runs backwards for 5 yards. Without slowing down or changing mechanics, he then turns to either the left or right and explodes to the first set of Marker Spots/cones, where the hand weights are released to allow the player to explode again to the outside Marker Spots/cones.

Key teaching points

- Maintain correct mechanics when running backwards, turning and running forwards (see pages 34–44)
- Increase the arm drive during the turn and acceleration phase
- Work off the balls of the feet, particularly when working backwards
- Release the arms without stopping or interrupting the arm mechanics

Sets and reps

2 sets of 6 reps, with a walk-back recovery between each rep and a 2-minute recovery between each set.

Variation/progression

The player works sideways for the first 5 metres (5 yards), then turns and explodes. Ensure that the sideways foot movements are short steps and not skips.

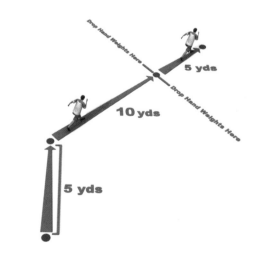

Figure 9.6 Attacking midfielders – turn and attack

DRILL | MIDFIELDERS – BALL CONTROL, FEED, TURN, RECEIVE AND SHOOT

Aim
To develop explosive turning and running skills. Midfielders often receive the ball while they are facing their own goal and use either their head, chest or feet to control it before quickly feeding it to a support player. The midfielder then turns and moves off at an angle to make himself available for the return pass that he receives before shooting at goal from 18–22 metres (20–25 yards).

Area/equipment
For maximum impact the drill should be performed in the relevant position on the pitch. Light hand weights and Marker Spots/cones placed as shown in figure 9.7.

Description
Working in pairs, Player 1 holds the hand weights and accelerates from Marker Spot/cone A towards the centre marker dot B. Player 2 at Marker Spot C delivers the ball to Player 1; Player 2 then moves off in an arcing run around either Marker Spot D or E. On receiving the ball, Player 1 lays it off into the path of Player 2's arcing run. Player 1 then turns explosively and accelerates down the centre of the grid towards the goal/markers. After 5 metres (5 yards), Player 1 releases the weights and Player 2 passes the ball into the path of Player 1, who explodes on to the ball and drives it into the goal.

Key teaching points
- Maintain correct mechanics in all directional running (see pages 34–44)
- Player 2 should use a powerful arm drive when making the arcing run – this helps his control
- Player 1 should use explosive arm drive during the turn phase and must not allow the feet to cross
- Encourage verbal and non-verbal communication between the players

Sets and reps
1 set of 8 reps, with a walk-back recovery between each rep.

Variations/progressions
- Player 1 commences the drill by moving sideways for the first 5 metres
- Player 2 also uses hand weights that are dropped half way through the arced run

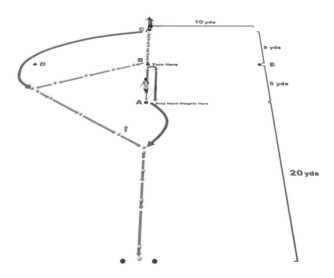

Figure 9.7 Midfielders – ball control, feed, turn, receive and shoot

DRILL

MIDFIELDERS –
ASSISTED AND RESISTED ARCING

Aim

To develop timed, explosive arced runs into the defensive area. Attacking midfielders who run well-timed, angled or arced runs in and around the penalty area are very difficult for defenders to pick up.

Area/equipment

For maximum impact the drill should be performed in the relevant position on the pitch. 2 Viper Belts and Marker Spots/cones. Place a Marker Spot/cone every 2 metres in an arc shape that is approximately 20 metres in length. Make several arcs and vary the directions and angles of these. (These should vary from session to session.) See figure 9.8.

Description

Working in pairs, both players wear Viper Belts and are attached one in front of the other by a flexi-cord, so that the lead runner is resisted from behind and the back runner is assisted by the lead runner. The lead runner sets off from the start and runs along the Marker Spots/cones. The flexi-cord will stretch after approximately 4–5 metres, at which point the back runner sets off. Alternate players between lead and back runner after each run and always finish a set with contrast runs.

Key teaching points

- Both players must maintain correct running form/mechanics (see pages 48–62)
- The assisted player should lean into the assistance – do not lean back
- Do not stretch the flexi-cord more than 2½ times its normal length

Sets and reps

1 set of 8 reps (i.e. 4 lead runs for each player), with a 90-second recovery between each rep and a 3-minute recovery before the next exercise.

Variation/progression

The lead runner runs backwards and turns after the back runner has started his explosive phase.

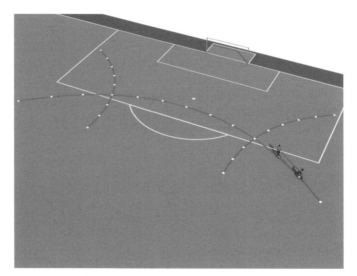

Figure 9.8 Midfielders – assisted and resisted arcing

DRILL	***ATTACKING MIDFIELDERS – OVERSPEED ARC RUNNING***
	POSITION SPECIFIC PATTERNS OF MOVEMENT DEVELOPMENT

Aim
One of the best weapons for an attacking midfielder is the ability to run on explosive arcs into the penalty area. This makes the player difficult to stop and defend against.

Area/equipment
For maximum impact the drill should be performed in the relevant position on the pitch. An Overspeed Tow Rope and Marker Spots/cones. Set out the markers to make arcs of approximately 36 metres in length, starting in the midfield and ending up somewhere in the penalty box. See figure 9.9.

Description
Work in groups of 3. Players 1 and 2 are attached by the Overspeed Tow Rope belts. Player 1 is resisted from the front and Player 2 is assisted from the back. Player 3 holds the handle and provides different levels of overspeed. Player 1 runs the arc and Player 2 runs in a straight line away from Player 3, who moves back towards the original start point of Player 1. Player 3 must also keep an eye on Player 1 to ensure that the right level of assistance is being provided.

Key teaching points
■ Players 1 and 2 must use correct running form/mechanics (see pages 48–62)
■ Player 1 must relax – do not resist the power
■ Player 1 should lean slightly in to the pull, not against it
■ Player 2 should take short, fast steps – do not sink into the hips
■ Player 3 must keep an eye on Player 1 – do not overload the power

Sets and reps
After 1 rep, rotate the players as follows: the resisted player becomes assisted, assisted becomes Player 3/control and Player 3/control becomes the resisted player. Each player to perform 5 reps in each position.

Variation/progression
This is an advanced variation. Player 1 swerves in and out of some Marker Spots/cones while running the arc.

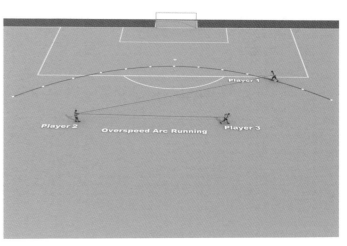

Figure 9.9 Attacking midfielders – overspeed arc running

DRILL FORWARDS – PEEL OFF AND TURN

Aim

Forwards can have little space in which to work, particularly when they are close to goal. The difference between scoring and missing can be a matter of centimetres; therefore, all forwards need to be explosive in all directions over the first 3–5 metres (3–5 yards). This drill will help to develop the movements required when a player has his back to the goal and is closely marked. The player peels off quickly to get into the space vacated by the defender to receive a pass and shoot for goal.

Area/equipment

For maximum impact the drill should be performed in the relevant position on the pitch. Viper Belt and 3 Marker Spots/cones marking out a line 8 metres long with a centre Marker Spot/cone 4 metres away from the start. See figure 9.10.

Description

Work in pairs. Player 1 wears the Viper Belt loosely around his waist to allow him to turn within the belt, and stands at Marker Spot/cone B. Player 2 holds the flexi-cord at Marker Spot/cone A. Player 1 accelerates explosively towards Marker Spot/cone C then swivels in the belt to explode back to Marker Spot/cone A.

Key teaching points

- Use an explosive arm drive
- Use short, explosive steps during the turn
- After the turn, lean into the assistance – do not lean back

Sets and reps

2 sets of 6 reps plus 1 contrast run, with a walk-back recovery between reps and a 3-minute recovery between sets.

Variation/progression

Player 2 has a ball and passes to Player 1 as he explodes back towards Marker Spot/cone A.

Figure 9.10 Forwards – peel off and turn

DRILL   FORWARDS – CROSS AND ATTACK GOAL

Aim

To develop short, explosive angled movements. Many forwards score goals by moving parallel to the goal, then darting in through a gap to strike or head a ball crossed over the face of the goal. Sometimes only the tiniest of touches is required to put the ball in the net. This drill has been developed to add explosion to the initial sideways and backwards movements that are used to confuse the defence, as well as the explosive, darting movement through a gap to contact the ball.

Area/equipment

For maximum impact the drill should be performed in the relevant position on the pitch. Viper Belt with 2 flexi-cords attached front and back and 7 Marker Spots/cones. Place 2 Marker Spots/cones 6 metres apart on the 6-yard line in front of the goal, and the other 5 Marker Spots/cones 2 metres away and in a straight line.

Description

Working in groups of 3, Player 1 wears the Viper Belt with a flexi-cord attached at the front that is held by Player 2. The second flexi-cord is attached at the back and held by Player 3. Player 1 stands between the 2 Marker Spots/cones on the 6-yard line, with Players 2 and 3 standing on Marker Spot/cones A and B respectively. On the coach's call, Player 1 explodes the 2 metres to a nominated Marker Spot/cone and then returns gently back to the start position for the next rep. See figure 9.11.

Key teaching points

■ Work off the balls of the feet
■ On the coach's call, use an explosive arm drive
■ The initial steps should be kept short, precise and explosive
■ The feet should be kept shoulder-width apart as much as possible This is crucial in case the player has to jump to contact the ball

Sets and reps

1 set of 8 reps plus 1 contrast run, with a walk-back recovery between reps and a 3-minute recovery before the next exercise.

Variations/progressions

■ Vary Player 1's starting position
■ Use a fourth player who nominates a Marker Spot/cone for Player 1 to explode on to before feeding the ball at different angles and heights for Player 1 to strike at goal

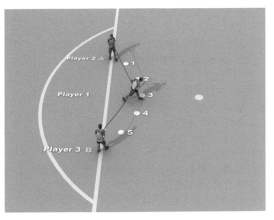

Figure 9.11 Forwards – cross and attack goal

DRILL
CENTRE FORWARD –
VERTICAL EXPLOSIVE HEADING POWER

Aim
To develop the centre forward's ability to explode as high as possible to meet crosses and direct them towards the goal.

Area/equipment
For maximum impact the drill should be performed in the relevant position on the pitch. Viper Belt with 3 flexi-cords (1 attached to each of the 3 anchor points) and 2 Marker Spots/cones placed 6 metres apart in front of goal on the 6-yard line.

Description
Players work in groups of 4. Player 1 (centre forward) wears the Viper Belt and stands in a central position between Marker Spots/cones A and B. Player 2 holds a flexi-cord on Marker Spot/cone A and Player 3 likewise at Marker Spot/cone B. Player 4 has the third flexi-cord, which is attached to the back of the Viper Belt, and stands approximately 4 metres away from Player 1 outside the 6-yard area (near the penalty spot). The coach throws the ball at different heights between Player 1 and the goal-line for Player 1 to head in to the goal. Player 1 returns to the start position after each rep. See figure 9.12.

Key teaching points
- Use explosive jump mechanics, especially arms for the take-off (see page 42)
- Players 2, 3 and 4 should remain seated on the ground for the duration of the drill to increase the resistance
- On landing, Player 1 must not sink into the hips
- Player 1 should try to stay upright and on the balls of the feet at all times

Sets and reps
1 set of 10 reps plus 2 contrast drills, with a walk-back recovery between reps and a 3-minute recovery before the next exercise.

Variation/progression
Introduce defenders in front of Player 1 to create a competitive jump/heading situation.

Figure 9.12 Centre forward – vertical explosive heading power

SAQ training for goalkeepers

Recent research has highlighted the importance of incorporating specific conditioning as a regular feature of a goalkeeper's training programme. Relying on the standard training methods used by outfield players fails to consider the specialist and specific conditioning required by goalkeepers. The demands placed on the goalkeeper are quite different to those placed on the outfield players. The ability to utilise the stretch and shortening cycle will have a positive impact on the explosive motion required while diving and springing into action.

Match analysis investigating the demands placed upon goalkeepers revealed the following (Whall and Kellet, 2001):

- 86 per cent of playing time was spent walking forwards, walking backwards or standing still

- the remaining 14 per cent of the time – equivalent to 12 minutes – required the goalkeepers on average to make 13 saves or intercept a number of crosses, and make 23 short 4–5-metre sprints

- many of the movements forwards, backwards and sideways indicated that a high level of multi-directional speed and agility was required

Additional research indicated that most goals are conceded in the second half, or after periods of high-intensity work when the goalkeeper's explosive abilities have been fatigued. Therefore, the ability of the goalkeeper to remain explosive and multi-directional throughout the game is crucial. The flying dive to the bottom corner to fingertip the ball around the post is vital not only in the first but also in the last minute of the game. In the English Premiership, almost 70 per cent of goals are scored in the bottom corners.

The following drills have been designed to ensure that goalkeepers become and remain explosive throughout the game. The drills in Chapters 7 and 8 (respectively, Vision and Reaction and Balance, Co-ordination, Feel and Judgement) are also highly recommended for goalkeepers.

DRILL GOALKEEPER – NARROWING THE ANGLES

Aim

To develop explosive acceleration and speed, balance and agility over the first 5–10 metres; to assist the goalkeeper in narrowing the angle of players' runs towards the goal and to cut out through-passes.

Area/equipment

For maximum impact the drill should be performed in the relevant position on the pitch. 4 short Fast Foot Ladders and 7–8 Marker Spots/cones. Place the 4 ladders just inside the 6-yard area and the Marker Spots/cones on the other side of the 6-yard line at different angles and distances of 5, 10 and 15 metres away from the ends of the ladders, as shown in figure 9.13(a).

Description

The coach nominates which ladder (A, B, C or D) the goalkeeper is to run down and which Marker Spots/cone (1–8) they are to attack. The goalkeeper explodes down the ladder then angles off and accelerates to the nominated Marker Spot/cone, where he sets himself for the save or dive.

Key teaching points

- The initial steps should be short and explosive
- Maintain a powerful arm drive
- Keep the head and eyes up
- Just before reaching the Marker Spot/cone, the goalkeeper should extend his arms and make himself look 'big'

Sets and reps

2 sets of 6 reps, with a walk-back recovery between each rep and a 3-minute recovery between each set.

Variations/progressions

- Introduce a ball to make the drill more goalkeeper-specific
- Replace the Marker Spots/cones with 1 or 2 players who move back and forth across the penalty area. The coach nominates the ladder for the goalkeeper to explode down; the goalkeeper then attempts to stop the outfield player who has just started his attack on goal
- The goalkeeper wears a Viper Belt which is attached to his partner by a safety belt on the opposite end of the flexi-cord. The partner stands behind the goalkeeper and works with them, but also creates a resistance throughout the drill
- Place 6 short ladders in a semi-circle around the goalkeeper and repeat the drill – see figure 9.13(b)

Figure 9.13(a) Goalkeeper – narrowing the angles

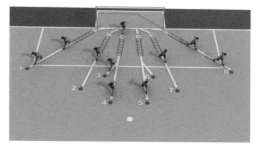

Figure 9.13(b) Goalkeeper – narrowing the angles – variation

DRILL

GOALKEEPER –
LATERAL SPEED DEVELOPMENT

Aim
To develop fast, controlled lateral movement across the goalmouth, making the goalkeeper difficult to get past and thus cutting down the options for the attacking players.

Area/equipment
For maximum impact the drill should be performed in the relevant position on the pitch. 2 Fast Foot Ladders and 6 balls. Place the ladders just in front of the goal line, leaving a small space between them where the goalkeeper will stand. Place the balls on a line parallel with the ladders approximately 1 yard away.

Description
The goalkeeper stands between the 2 ladders. On the coach's call he commences lateral fast-foot drills (see pages 71–83) to either the left or right. The coach then nominates a ball (1, 2 or 3) and the goalkeeper explodes out of the ladder and on to the ball. See figure 9.14.

Key teaching points
■ Stay tall during the lateral drills
■ Use a few quick arm drives then revert to a 'ready' position, i.e. arms and hands extended as if to save the ball
■ Keep the head and eyes up

Sets and reps
2 sets of 6 reps, with a walk-back recovery between each rep and a 3-minute recovery between each set.

Variations/progressions
■ Position 2 players just outside the 6-yard area, 1 on each side. On the coach's call the goalkeeper and the relevant player both attack the same ball
■ The goalkeeper wears a Viper Belt with 2 flexi-cords attached to players standing on either side of the goal in order to work the player under resistance

Figure 9.14 Goalkeeper – lateral speed development

DRILL   GOALKEEPER – EXPLOSIVE DIVING

Aim
To develop multi-directional explosive diving, making the goalkeeper virtually unbeatable.

Area/equipment
For maximum impact the drill should be performed in the relevant position on the pitch. Balls and a Viper Belt with 2 flexi-cords attached one on either side. The other end of the flexi-cord should be attached to either goalpost at waist height.

Description
The goalkeeper wears the belt and stands in the centre of the goal. The coach stands with the balls in the centre of the 6-yard line, then sends the balls towards the goal at different angles and heights. The goalkeeper attempts to save these by moving explosively in the appropriate direction before recovering and setting himself up again in position to repeat the drill. See figure 9.15.

Key teaching points
- The goalkeeper should use short and explosive steps
- Do not sink into the hips
- Stay tall and 'big'
- Keep the head and eyes up
- Work off the balls of the feet at all times
- Keep the shoulders relaxed

Sets and reps
2 set of 10 reps plus 2 contrast saves, with a walk-back recovery between each rep and a 3-minute recovery between each set.

Variation/progression
Introduce 2 saves per repetition.

Figure 9.15 Goalkeeper – explosive diving

DRILL

GOALKEEPER –
ACCELERATION AND JUMP DRILL

Aim

To develop explosive speed over a short distance and an explosive vertical jump. The ability to do this will allow the goalkeeper to cut down space in danger areas and control balls crossed and floated into this area.

Area/equipment

For maximum impact the drill should be performed in the relevant position on the pitch. A Viper Belt with 2 flexi-cords attached one on either side, and 6 Marker Spots/cones. Place 2 starting Marker Spots/cones (A and B) 3 metres (3 yards) away from the goal line. The remaining 4 Marker Spots/cones are placed 3–4 metres away, i.e. on or just over the 6-yard line, at different angles.

Description

Working in pairs the goalkeeper wears the Viper Belt and the other player stands behind the goal line holding both the flexi-cords. The coach then nominates a Marker Spot/cone and the goalkeeper accelerates towards it. On reaching that Marker Spot/cone, he either dives or jumps into the air. On landing, he jockeys quickly back to the start position to await the next instruction. See figure 9.16.

Key teaching points

- The goalkeeper should use short and explosive steps
- The goalkeeper should stay tall and keep his head and eyes up
- The player holding the flexi-cords should remain in a static, crouched position to increase the level of resistance

Sets and reps

2 sets of 10 reps plus 2 contrast runs, with the backward jockey as the recovery between each rep and a 3-minute recovery between each set.

Variations/progressions

- Work the goalkeeper laterally by turning the belt around and working sideways on to the Marker Spots/cones. Ensure that the goalkeeper uses short, sharp steps and not skips
- At the nominated Marker Spot/cone the goalkeeper makes 2 saves (1 high and 1 low) before jockeying backwards to the start position

Figure 9.16 Goalkeeper – acceleration and jump drill

DRILL   *GOALKEEPER –*
EXPLOSIVE GROUND REACTIONS

Aim

To develop explosive 'get-ups' for goalkeepers who have just performed a save, and are on the ground and have to get up as quickly as possible to initiate another save or block.

Area/equipment

For maximum impact the drill should be performed in the relevant position on the pitch. Jelly Balls (or medicine balls). Use various weights depending on the age group that you are working with. Seniors should use 7–11 kg balls.

Description

The goalkeeper lies on his back holding a Jelly Ball (or medicine ball) to his chest. On the coach's call, the goalkeeper simultaneously gets up and throws the jelly ball away, finishing the drill in a 'ready' position.

Key teaching points

- Try to make the 'get-up' one continuous movement (see page 97)
- Try to get onto the balls of the feet as quickly as possible

Sets and reps

3 sets of 10 reps plus 1 contrast without the Jelly Ball, with the return to the start position as the recovery between reps and a 3-minute recovery between each set.

Variations/progressions

- Vary the start position, i.e. side, knees, turn, etc.
- Introduce a ball for the goalkeeper to save as soon as he has got to his feet
- Repeat the drill as above but with the goalkeeper sitting on an Agility Disc

DRILL GOALKEEPER – BUNT BAT DRILL

Aim
To develop lightning-quick hand–eye co-ordination.

Area/equipment
Indoor or outdoor area. A Bunt Bat (or a stick with 3 different-coloured tapes at each end and in the middle) and tennis balls, foam balls or beanbags.

Description
Working in pairs, one of the goalkeepers holds the Bunt Bat. His partner stands approximately 3–4 metres away and throws a ball or beanbag and simultaneously calls the colour of one of the balls on the Bunt Bat. The goalkeeper's task is to fend off the ball/beanbag with the appropriate coloured ball on the Bunt Bat. See figure 9.17.

Key teaching points
- Start throwing the balls or beanbags slowly and gradually build up speed
- The goalkeeper should be in a 'set' position

Sets and reps
3 sets of 25 reps, with a 30-second recovery between each set.

Variations/progressions
- Use different-coloured balls/beanbags – when the ball/beanbag has been thrown, it is to be fended off with the corresponding coloured ball on the Bunt Bat
- The goalkeeper stands on an Agility Disc while performing the drill

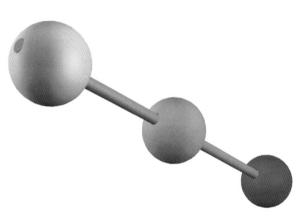

Figure 9.17 Goalkeeper – Bunt Bat drill

DRILL GOALKEEPER – FAST HANDS

Aim
To develop lightning-quick hand reactions.

Area/equipment
Indoor or outdoor area.

Description
Working in pairs, Player 1 puts his hands together and holds them slightly away in front of the chest. Player 2 stands directly in front with his hands held at the side. The drill begins with Player 2 attempting to slap Player 1's hands. Player 1 tries to prevent Player 2 by moving his hands away as quickly as possible. Players alternate roles.

Key teaching points
■ Stand in an athletic position
■ Keep the head still

Sets and reps
30 seconds each per drill.

Variations/progressions
■ Player 1 holds his hands out with the palms facing the ground, the tips of the thumbs just touching. Player 2 holds his hands just above. The drill commences with player 2 attempting to slap both of Player 1's hands before Player 1 can react by moving them away
■ Player 1 stands directly in front of Player 2, 1 or 2 metres apart. Player 1 jabs a punch at Player 2, who attempts to clap both hands over the fist

CHAPTER 10 WARM-DOWN AND RECOVERY

DYNAMIC FLEX™ DRILLS TO IMPROVE SUPPLENESS AND DYNAMIC RANGE OF MOVEMENT IN ORDER TO MAXIMISE RECOVERY AND IMPROVE TRAINING PERFORMANCE

The importance of an effective recovery must not be under-estimated. Once training or a game is completed, the goal must be to recover the players as quickly as possible for the next bout of intensive activity, whether that is the next training session or another game. The following recovery techniques are recommended:

Active warm-down

Perform reverse Dynamic Flex for 5–7 minutes, gradually decreasing the range of movements and intensity. This will help to:

■ disperse lactic acid

■ prevent blood pooling in the lower body

■ return the body systems to normal levels

■ assist in recovery

In the reverse Dynamic Flex warm-down, movements gradually become less intense and smaller in amplitude (like a warm-up in reverse). It is crucial that these exercises still focus on quality movement and good mechanics.

Static stretches (non-compulsory)

If you wish to perform static stretches, now would be the best time to implement them. The static stretches to be incorporated should mirror the movements being carried out in the warm-down.

Ice baths, cold baths or cold showers

Recent research has indicated the beneficial properties of cryogenic therapy (ice/cold) to aid recovery. The following guidelines should be followed:

ICE BATH
3 x 3 minutes with a 3-minute recovery between ice baths.

COLD BATH
2 x 5 minutes with a 3-minute recovery between baths.

COLD SHOWER
10 minutes constant.

Nutrition

This is a great time to start replenishing the body's energy systems with effective recovery fluids and nutritional aids.

DRILL HIGH KNEE-LIFT SKIP

Follow the instructions on page 12.

Aim
To warm down the hips and buttocks gradually.

Sets and reps
2 x 18 metres, 1 forwards and 1 backwards.

Intensity
60 per cent for the first 18 metres and 50 per cent for the second 18 metres.

DRILL KNEE-ACROSS SKIP

Follow the instructions on page 13.

Aim
To warm down the hip flexors gradually by lowering the intensity of the exercise.

Sets and reps
2 x 18 metres, 1 forwards and 1 backwards.

Intensity
50 per cent for the first 18 metres and 40 per cent for the second 18 metres.

DRILL WIDE SKIPS

Follow the instructions on page 10.

Aim
To warm down the hips and ankles.

Sets and reps
2 x 18 metres, 1 forwards and 1 backwards.

Intensity
40 per cent for the first 18 metres and 30 per cent for the second 18 metres.

DRILL CARIOCA

Follow the instructions on page 23.

Aim
To warm down the hips and bring the core body temperature down.

Sets and reps
2 x 18 metres, 1 left leg leading and 1 right leg leading.

Intensity
30 per cent for the first 18 metres and 20 per cent for the second 18 metres.

DRILL   *SMALL SKIPS*

Follow the instructions on page 9.

Aim
To warm down the muscles of the lower leg and the ankle.

Sets and reps
2 x 18 metres, 1 forwards and 1 backwards.

Intensity
20 per cent for the first 18 metres and 10 per cent for the second 18 metres.

DRILL   *ANKLE FLICKS*

Follow the instructions on page 8.

Aim
To bring the heart rate down and to stretch the calf and the ankle.

Sets and reps
2 x 18 metres, 1 forwards and 1 backwards.

Intensity
10 per cent for the first 18 metres and then walking flicks for the second 18 metres.

DRILL   *HURDLE WALK*

Follow the instructions on page 20.

Aim
To bring the heart rate down.

Sets and reps
2 x 18 metres, 1 forwards and 1 backwards.

Intensity
Walking.

DRILL   *WALKING HAMSTRING*

Follow the instructions on page 21.

Aim
To stretch the back of the thigh.

Sets and reps
2 x 18 metres, 1 forwards and 1 backwards.

Intensity
Walking.

insert pic 0133

DRILL   *LATISSIMUS DORSI STRETCH*

Aim
To stretch the muscles in the back.

Description
Stand in an upright position and link the hands together in front of the chest. Then push the hands out, straightening the arms and arching the back forwards.

Key teaching points
- Do not force the arms out too far
- Focus on slow, controlled breathing

Sets and reps
Hold the stretch for approximately 10 seconds.

DRILL   *QUADRICEPS STRETCH*

Aim
To stretch and assist the recovery of the thigh muscles.

Description
Stand on one leg and bring the heel of the raised foot in towards the buttock. Using the hand of that side, hold the 'lace' area of that foot and squeeze it in to the buttock.

Key teaching points
- Try to keep the knees together
- Ensure the support leg is slightly bent. Repeat on the opposite leg
- Press the hip forwards
- Focus on slow, controlled breathing
- Do not force the stretch – just squeeze it in gently

Sets and reps
Hold the stretch for approximately 10 seconds on each leg.

Variation
The exercise can be performed while the player is lying down sideways on the floor.

DRILL   *HAMSTRING STRETCH*

Aim
To stretch and assist the recovery of the hamstring at the back of the thigh.

Description
Sit on the floor with one leg extended and the other leg bent. Bend forwards from the hips and reach down towards the foot.

Key teaching points
- Focus on slow, controlled breathing
- Bend forwards from the hip
- Keep the back straight and flat
- Flex the foot to increase the stretch

Sets and reps
Hold the stretch for approximately 10 seconds on each leg.

DRILL   *ADDUCTORS STRETCH*

Aim
To stretch and assist the recovery of the adductor muscles of the inner thigh.

Description
Stand with the legs apart, bend one knee and keep the foot at a 45-degree angle to the body, toes pointing ahead and knee over the ankle. The other leg should be straight. Repeat on the opposite leg.

Key teaching points
- Focus on slow, controlled breathing.
- Do not force the stretch
- Keep the back straight
- Do not allow the knee of the bent leg to go beyond the toes

Sets and reps
Hold the stretch for approximately 10 seconds on each leg.

DRILL   *CALF STRETCH*

Aim
To stretch and assist the recovery of the calf muscles.

Description
Stand with the legs split and both feet pointing forwards, one leg to the front and the other to the back. The weight should be transferred to the knee of the front leg.

Key teaching points
- The front knee should move to a position over the ankle, never beyond the toes
- The back leg should be kept straight; it is this calf that will be stretched. Repeat on the other side
- Focus on slow, controlled breathing
- Do not force the stretch
- Apply the weight slowly to the front foot

Sets and reps
Hold the stretch for approximately 10 seconds on each leg.

CHAPTER 11

THE SAQ FOOTBALL PROGRAMME

PLANNING AND INTEGRATING SAQ TRAINING INTO A FOOTBALL-SPECIFIC PROGRAMME

The following chapter provides sample training sessions and programmes for both professional and amateur teams, with a focus on pre- and in-season sessions.

The art of any programme is how it is periodised throughout the year, plus its ability to recognise individual needs and accommodate unscheduled changes. The best programmes are those that have variation, provide challenges, keep players on their toes and accept individuality. Too much of the 'same' demotivates individuals and teams, so that performance may be compromised.

Some simple rules

- Start with dynamic flexibility

- Explosive work and sprints should be completed early in the session, before endurance work

- Plan sessions so that an explosive day is followed by a preparation day

- Progress from simple drills to complex drills.

- Don't restrict programmes to one-week periods; work with different blocks of 4–8–10–12 days

- Teach one new skill a day

- Rest and recovery periods must be well planned

- Vary work:rest ratios in order to increase the intensity of the work rate

- Build up strength before performing plyometrics

- Keep sessions short and sharp. Explanation and discussions should be conducted before and afterwards, not in activity time

- Finish off each session with static (PNF) stretching

Pre–season training

Mention the words 'pre-season training' to most players and you will get a look of horror. For years, coaches and trainers have been fixated by the development of the aerobic energy system by utilising long, slow, steady-state runs from 8 km to anything up to 12 km. In fact, research clearly states that this type of activity is not suitable for football players – and is actually likely to make them slower and cause unnecessary injuries.

Most activity in football lasts for an average of 4–6 seconds, and for about 18–22 metres in distance. Football is a start–stop game, which utilises fast-twitch fibres and primarily depends on the anaerobic system (see Glossary of terms, page 199). By training the anaerobic system via explosive drills like those in this programme, players will benefit in a wide range of ways, including:

- an increased ability to tolerate higher levels of lactic acid – a by-product of high-intensity activity

- an increase in aerobic power, which is the energy system that uses oxygen without turning off the fast twitch fibres, vital because it is these that enable footballers to perform explosive multi-directional movements such as sprinting, jumping, tackling and diving

- an improved recovery time – both of which will enable players to play harder and for longer

So it's simple – long, slow runs do not emulate what happens on the field; they are not specific to football. Instead intermittent, intensive runs of various work:rest ratios – including side-steps, swerves, backward movements and jumps – better prepare your players for the demands of the game.

Professional programme

The pre-season professional programmes start with a higher percentage of time spent on running mechanics than explosive work. As the season draws closer the emphasis progressively changes with a higher percentage of time being spent on explosive development and less on the mechanics.

By gradually shortening the recovery periods and increasing the intensity of the interval runs the programme becomes more game-like in intensity. By incorporating competitive football conditioning teamwork exercises in the latter part of the pre-season programme, the players are prepared for the psychological and physical demands of the forthcoming competitive season.

The professional in-season programmes have been designed for use as a continuous top-up of the pre-season work already started. The importance of in-season programmes is to ensure that the players remain fresh, motivated and match-fit.

Amateur programme

Training for amateur football differs from training for the professional game, predominantly in the amount of time available for preparation. Amateur players are part-time and have to rely more heavily on personal training programmes away from the club. This fact has been allowed for within the programmes on the following pages.

The amateur pre-season programmes also use interval-based training where the work, rest and recovery ratios can be manipulated by the coach. In this way the coach can ensure that, at the end of the pre-season phase, a higher intensity of training has been achieved in preparation for the season itself.

As with the professional programmes, the amateur in-season programmes have been designed to keep the players match-fit, motivated and fresh for all games.

PRE–SEASON: PROFESSIONAL

T U E S D A Y

DYNAMIC FLEX WARM-UP	15 min
MECHANICS	15 min
Hurdles, Fast Foot Ladder drills	
To develop and perfect the correct linear, lateral and vertical movement mechanics; to increase foot speed and stride frequency	
VISION AND REACTION TRAINING	5 min
FOOTBALL-SPECIFIC CONDITIONING	25 min
Innervation	
Football-related movement drills: agility, speed, multi-directional	
Explosion	
Resisted, random agility and assisted drills. Ratio: mechanics 70%; explosive 30%. Active recovery	
To develop multi-directional speed	
FOOTBALL-SPECIFIC ENDURANCE	20 min
Sprint endurance work. Example: 10 x 80 m, 8 x 60 m, 6 x 40 m. Timed active recovery	
WARM-DOWN/STATIC STRETCHING	10 min
Preparation for afternoon session	

Total: 90 min

WEDNESDAY

DYNAMIC FLEX WARM-UP	15 min
MECHANICS Hurdles, Fast Foot Ladder drills To develop and perfect the correct linear, lateral and vertical movement mechanics; to increase foot speed and stride frequency	15 min
VISION AND REACTION TRAINING	5 min
FOOTBALL-SPECIFIC CONDITIONING **Innervation** Football-related movement drills: agility, speed, multi-directional **Explosion** Resisted, random agility and assisted drills. Ratio: mechanics 70%; explosive 30%. Active recovery To develop multi-directional speed	25 min
FOOTBALL-SPECIFIC ENDURANCE SAQ combination runs. 3 circuits – timed	20 min
WARM-DOWN/STATIC STRETCHING Preparation for afternoon session	10 min

Total: 90 min

THURSDAY

DYNAMIC FLEX WARM-UP	15 min
MECHANICS	15 min
Hurdles, Fast Foot Ladder drills	
To develop and perfect the correct linear, lateral and vertical movement mechanics; to increase foot speed and stride frequency	
VISION AND REACTION TRAINING	5 min
FOOTBALL-SPECIFIC CONDITIONING	25 min
Innervation	
Football-related movement drills: agility, speed, multi-directional	
Explosion	
Resisted, random agility and assisted drills. Ratio: mechanics 70%; explosive 30%. Active recovery	
To develop multi-directional speed	
FOOTBALL-SPECIFIC ENDURANCE	20 min
Sprint endurance work. Example: 10 x 80 m, 8 x 60 m, 6 x 40 m. Timed active recovery	
WARM-DOWN/STATIC STRETCHING	10 min
Preparation for afternoon session	

Total: 90 min

FRIDAY

DYNAMIC FLEX WARM-UP	15 min
MECHANICS	15 min
Hurdles, Fast Foot Ladder drills	
To develop and perfect the correct linear, lateral and vertical movement mechanics; to increase foot speed and stride frequency	
VISION AND REACTION TRAINING	5 min
FOOTBALL-SPECIFIC CONDITIONING	25 min
Innervation	
Football-related movement drills: agility, speed, multi-directional	
Explosion	
Resisted, random agility and assisted drills	
To develop explosive multi-directional speed. Ratio: mechanics 60%, explosive 40%. Active recovery	
FOOTBALL-SPECIFIC ENDURANCE	20 min
SAQ combination runs. 3 circuits – timed	
WARM-DOWN/STATIC STRETCHING	10 min
Preparation for afternoon session	

Total: 90 min

S A T U R D A Y

DYNAMIC FLEX WARM-UP	20 min
MECHANICS	15 min
Fast Foot Ladder and hurdles	
VISION AND REACTION TRAINING	5 min
COMPETITIVE FOOTBALL CONDITIONING	40 min
Group splits into teams. Non-contact competitive football movements, drills, games and challenges will be used to increase pressure:	

- relays

- obstacle courses

- competition games

- testing

To develop sprint, reactions and include enjoyment factor. Psychological impact: will increase competitiveness

WARM-DOWN/STATIC STRETCHING	10 min
Preparation for afternoon session	

Total: 90 min

SUNDAY/MONDAY

Two day recovery, personal stretching/swimming

TUESDAY

DYNAMIC FLEX WARM-UP	15 min
MECHANICS	15 min
Hurdles, Fast Foot Ladder drills	
To develop and perfect the correct linear, lateral and vertical movement mechanics; to increase foot speed and stride frequency	
VISION AND REACTION TRAINING	5 min
FOOTBALL-SPECIFIC CONDITIONING	25 min
Innervation	
Football-related movement drills: agility, speed, multi-directional	
Explosion	
Resisted, random agility and assisted drills. Ratio: mechanics 60%; explosive 40%. Active recovery	
To develop multi-directional speed	
FOOTBALL-SPECIFIC ENDURANCE	20 min
Sprint endurance work. Example: 10 x 80 m, 8 x 60 m, 6 x 40 m. Timed active recovery	
WARM-DOWN/STATIC STRETCHING	10 min
Preparation for afternoon session	

Total: 90 min

WEDNESDAY

DYNAMIC FLEX WARM-UP	15 min
MECHANICS	15 min
Hurdles, Fast Foot Ladder drills	
To develop and perfect the correct linear, lateral and vertical movement mechanics; to increase foot speed and stride frequency	
VISION AND REACTION TRAINING	5 min
FOOTBALL-SPECIFIC CONDITIONING	25 min
Innervation	
Football-related movement drills: agility, speed, multi-directional	
Explosion	
Resisted, random agility and assisted drills. Ratio: mechanics 60%; explosive 40%. Active recovery	
To develop multi-directional speed	
FOOTBALL-SPECIFIC ENDURANCE	20 min
SAQ combination runs. Volume increased: 4 circuits – each timed	
WARM-DOWN/STATIC STRETCHING	10 min
Preparation for afternoon session	
Evening pool session	

Total: 90 min

THURSDAY

DYNAMIC FLEX WARM-UP	15 min
MECHANICS	15 min
Hurdles, Fast Foot Ladder drills	
To develop and perfect the correct linear, lateral and vertical movement mechanics; to increase foot speed and stride frequency	
VISION AND REACTION TRAINING	5 min
FOOTBALL-SPECIFIC CONDITIONING	25 min
Innervation	
Football-related movement drills: agility, speed, multi-directional	
Explosion	
Resisted, random agility and assisted drills	
To develop multi-directional speed. Ratio: mechanics 60%, explosive 40%. Active recovery	
FOOTBALL-SPECIFIC ENDURANCE	20 min
Sprint endurance work. Example: 11 x 80 m, 10 x 60 m, 8 x 40 m. Sprint volume increased. Timed active recovery	
WARM-DOWN/STATIC STRETCHING	10 min
Preparation for afternoon session	

Total: 90 min

F R I D A Y

DYNAMIC FLEX WARM-UP	15 min
MECHANICS	15 min
Hurdles, Fast Foot Ladder drills	
To develop and perfect the correct linear, lateral and vertical movement mechanics; to increase foot speed and stride frequency	
VISION AND REACTION TRAINING	5 min
FOOTBALL-SPECIFIC CONDITIONING	25 min
Innervation	
Football-related movement drills: agility, speed, multi-directional	
Explosion	
Resisted, random agility and assisted drills	
To develop explosive multi-directional speed. Ratio: mechanics 50%, explosive 50%. Active recovery	
FOOTBALL-SPECIFIC ENDURANCE	20 min
SAQ combination runs. 4 circuits – timed	
WARM-DOWN/STATIC STRETCHING	10 min
Preparation for afternoon session	

Total: 90 min

SATURDAY

DYNAMIC FLEX WARM-UP	20 min
COMPETITIVE FOOTBALL CONDITIONING Group splits into teams. Non-contact competitive football movements, drills, games and challenges will be used to increase pressure: ■ relays ■ obstacle courses ■ competition games ■ testing To develop sprint, reactions and include enjoyment factor. Psychological impact: will increase competitiveness	40 min
WARM-DOWN/STATIC STRETCHING Preparation for afternoon session	10 min

Total: 70 min

SUNDAY / MONDAY

Two day recovery, personal stretching/swimming

TUESDAY

DYNAMIC FLEX WARM-UP	15 min
MECHANICS	15 min
Hurdles, Fast Foot Ladder drills	
To develop and perfect the correct linear, lateral and vertical movement mechanics; to increase foot speed and stride frequency	
VISION AND REACTION TRAINING	5 min
FOOTBALL-SPECIFIC CONDITIONING	25 min
Innervation	
Football-related movement drills: agility, speed, multi-directional	
Explosion	
Resisted, random agility and assisted drills. Ratio: mechanics 50%; explosive 50%. Active recovery	
To develop multi-directional speed	
FOOTBALL-SPECIFIC ENDURANCE	20 min
Sprint endurance work. Example: 11 x 80 m, 10 x 60 m, 8 x 40 m. Active recovery time reduced	
WARM-DOWN/STATIC STRETCHING	10 min
Preparation for afternoon session	

Total: 90 min

WEDNESDAY

DYNAMIC FLEX WARM-UP	15 min
MECHANICS	15 min
Hurdles, Fast Foot Ladder drills	
To develop and perfect the correct linear, lateral and vertical movement mechanics; to increase foot speed and stride frequency	
VISION AND REACTION TRAINING	5 min
FOOTBALL-SPECIFIC CONDITIONING	25 min
Innervation	
Football-related movement drills: agility, speed, multi-directional	
Explosion	
Resisted, random agility and assisted drills.	
To develop explosive multi-directional speed. Ratio: mechanics 40%, explosive 60%. Active recovery	
FOOTBALL-SPECIFIC ENDURANCE	20 min
SAQ combination runs. 4 circuits – timed	
WARM-DOWN/STATIC STRETCHING	10 min
Preparation for afternoon session	

Total: 90 min

THURSDAY

DYNAMIC FLEX WARM-UP	15 min
MECHANICS Hurdles, Fast Foot Ladder drills To develop and perfect the correct linear, lateral and vertical movement mechanics; to increase foot speed and stride frequency	15 min
VISION AND REACTION TRAINING	5 min
FOOTBALL-SPECIFIC CONDITIONING **Innervation** Football-related movement drills: agility, speed, multi-directional **Explosion** Resisted, random agility and assisted drills To develop multi-directional speed. Ratio: mechanics 40%, explosive 60%. Active recovery	25 min
FOOTBALL-SPECIFIC ENDURANCE Sprint endurance work. Example: 12 x 80 m, 10 x 60 m, 10 x 40 m. Sprint volume increased. Timed active recovery	20 min
WARM-DOWN/STATIC STRETCHING Preparation for afternoon session	10 min

Total: 90 min

FRIDAY

DYNAMIC FLEX WARM-UP	15 min
MECHANICS	15 min
Hurdles, Fast Foot Ladder drills	
To develop and perfect the correct linear, lateral and vertical movement mechanics; to increase foot speed and stride frequency	
VISION AND REACTION TRAINING	5 min
FOOTBALL-SPECIFIC CONDITIONING	25 min
Innervation	
Football-related movement drills: agility, speed, multi-directional	
Explosion	
Resisted, random agility and assisted drills	
To develop explosive multi-directional speed. Ratio: mechanics 40%, explosive 60%. Active recovery	
FOOTBALL-SPECIFIC ENDURANCE	20 min
SAQ combination runs. 4 circuits – timed	
WARM-DOWN/STATIC STRETCHING	10 min
Preparation for afternoon session	
Evening pool session	

Total: 90 min

SATURDAY

DYNAMIC FLEX WARM-UP	20 min
COMPETITIVE FOOTBALL CONDITIONING Group splits into teams. Non-contact competitive football movements, drills, games and challenges will be used to increase pressure: ■ relays ■ obstacle courses ■ competition games ■ testing To develop sprint, reactions and include enjoyment factor Psychological impact: will increase competitiveness	40 min
WARM-DOWN/STATIC STRETCHING Preparation for afternoon session	10 min

Total: 70 min

TUESDAY

DYNAMIC FLEX WARM-UP	15 min
MECHANICS	15 min
Hurdles, Fast Foot Ladder drills	
To develop and perfect the correct linear, lateral and vertical movement mechanics; to increase foot speed and stride frequency	
VISION AND REACTION TRAINING	5 min
FOOTBALL-SPECIFIC CONDITIONING	25 min
Innervation	
Football-related movement drills: agility, speed, multi-directional	
Explosion	
Resisted, random agility and assisted drills	
To develop multi-directional speed. Ratio: mechanics 30%, explosive 70%. Active recovery	
FOOTBALL-SPECIFIC ENDURANCE	20 min
Sprint endurance work. Example: 12 x 80 m, 10 x 60 m, 10 x 40 m. Active timed recovery reduced	
WARM-DOWN/STATIC STRETCHING	10 min
Preparation for afternoon session	

Total: 90 min

WEDNESDAY

DYNAMIC FLEX WARM-UP	15 min
MECHANICS	15 min
Hurdles, Fast Foot Ladder drills	
To develop and perfect the correct linear, lateral and vertical movement mechanics; to increase foot speed and stride frequency	
VISION AND REACTION TRAINING	5 min
FOOTBALL-SPECIFIC CONDITIONING	25 min
Innervation	
Football-related movement drills: agility, speed, multi-directional	
Explosion	
Resisted, random agility and assisted drills	
To develop explosive multi-directional speed. Ratio: mechanics 30%, explosive 70%. Active recovery	
FOOTBALL-SPECIFIC ENDURANCE	20 min
SAQ combination runs. Volume increased. 5 circuits – timed	
WARM-DOWN/STATIC STRETCHING	10 min
Preparation for afternoon session	

Total: 90 min

THURSDAY

DYNAMIC FLEX WARM-UP	15 min
MECHANICS	15 min
Hurdles, Fast Foot Ladder drills	
To develop and perfect the correct linear, lateral and vertical movement mechanics; to increase foot speed and stride frequency	
VISION AND REACTION TRAINING	5 min
FOOTBALL-SPECIFIC CONDITIONING	25 min
Innervation	
Football-related movement drills: agility, speed, multi-directional	
Explosion	
Resisted, random agility and assisted drills	
To develop multi-directional speed. Ratio: mechanics 30%, explosive 70%. Active recovery	
FOOTBALL-SPECIFIC ENDURANCE	20 min
Sprint endurance work. Example: 12 x 80 m, 12 x 60 m, 12 x 40 m. Sprint volume increased. Timed active recovery	
WARM-DOWN/STATIC STRETCHING	10 min
Preparation for afternoon session	

Total: 90 min

F R I D A Y

DYNAMIC FLEX WARM-UP	15 min
MECHANICS	15 min
Hurdles, Fast Foot Ladder drills	
To develop and perfect the correct linear, lateral and vertical movement mechanics; to increase foot speed and stride frequency	
VISION AND REACTION TRAINING	5 min
FOOTBALL-SPECIFIC CONDITIONING	25 min
Innervation	
Football-related movement drills: agility, speed, multi-directional	
Explosion	
Resisted, random agility and assisted drills	
To develop explosive multi-directional speed. Ratio: mechanics 30%, explosive 70%. Active recovery	
FOOTBALL-SPECIFIC ENDURANCE	20 min
SAQ combination runs. 5 circuits – timed	
WARM-DOWN/STATIC STRETCHING	10 min
Preparation for afternoon session	

Total: 90 min

SATURDAY

DYNAMIC FLEX WARM-UP	20 min
COMPETITIVE FOOTBALL CONDITIONING Group splits into teams. Non-contact competitive football movements, drills, games and challenges will be used to increase pressure: ■ relays ■ obstacle courses ■ competition games ■ testing To develop sprint, reactions and include enjoyment factor. Psychological impact: will increase competitiveness	40 min
WARM-DOWN/STATIC STRETCHING Preparation for afternoon session	10 min

Total: 70 min

IN–SEASON: PROFESSIONAL

SATURDAY OR ONE GAME A WEEK

All sessions start with Dynamic Flex.

	a.m.		p.m.	
SUNDAY	Pool recovery, static stretching	45 min	Recovery	
MONDAY	**SAQ session** Resistance work for power Ball work	90 min	Strength/power	45 min
TUESDAY	**SAQ session** Fast feet Mechanics Agility Speed work Ball work	90 min	Recovery	
WEDNESDAY	**SAQ session** Resistance work for power Ball work	90 min	Personal circuit conditioning	60 min
THURSDAY	**SAQ session** Fast feet Mechanics Agility Ball work	75 min	Recovery	
FRIDAY	Dynamic Flex	15 min	Rest	
SATURDAY	Dynamic Flex, **game**, warm-down		Rejuvenate, refuel	

N.B.: *rest* – feet up and do nothing; *recovery* – active, low-intensity recovery, e.g. swimming, walking, stretching, sauna, spa, massage; *rejuvenate* – immediately after game, refuelling and re-hydrating.

TWO GAMES A WEEK

All sessions start with Dynamic Flex.

	a.m.		p.m.	
SUNDAY	Pool recovery		Light ball work Stretching	45 min
MONDAY	Moderate strength/power **SAQ session** Agility Fast feet Ball work	60 min	Light power	35 min
TUESDAY	Rest		Dynamic Flex warm-up to include fast feet work, **game**, cool-down and rejuvenate	
WEDNESDAY	Rejuvenate		Ball work	
THURSDAY	**SAQ session** Fast feet Mechanics Agility	45 min	Personal circuit	45 min
FRIDAY	Dynamic Flex Light ball work	60 min	Rest	
SATURDAY	Dynamic Flex, **game**, warm-down		Rejuvenate, refuel	

PRE–SEASON: AMATEUR

1 4 - D A Y   C Y C L E

N.B.: Time in brackets indicates recovery period before moving on to next element of session.
All sessions start with Dynamic Flex.

MONDAY	Personal weights programme, flexibility work	
TUESDAY	**SAQ session** Dynamic Flex *Interval work:* Combination run Football drills Combination run Football drills Combination run Football drills Abdominal ball workout, core development, warm-down and static stretching	**40 min** 15 min 5 min (2 min) 5 min (2 min) 5 min (2 min) 5 min (2 min) 5 min (2 min) 5 min (2 min) 15 min total
WEDNESDAY	Active recovery, swimming, stretch	
THURSDAY	**SAQ session** Dynamic Flex with ball Power work with Jelly Balls Interval running Football drills Interval running Football drills Interval running Football drills Warm-down and static stretching	**40 min** 15 min – 5 min (2 min) 5 min (2 min) 5 min (2 min) 5 min (2 min) 5 min (2 min) 5 min (2 min) 15 min total
FRIDAY	Personal weights programme Stretch, swim, sauna	
SATURDAY	**SAQ session** Dynamic Flex with ball Power development including recovery Football drills Football-specific runs Warm-down stretch then swim	 15 min 40 min (3 min) 40 min (3 min) 20 min 15 min total + swim
SUNDAY	Stretch – rest	
MONDAY	Personal weights programme, flexibility work	

14-DAY CYCLE cont.

TUESDAY	**SAQ session**	**40 min**
	Dynamic Flex	15 min
	Interval work:	
	Combination run	5 min (2 min)
	Football drills	5 min (2 min)
	Combination run	5 min (2 min)
	Football drills	5 min (2 min)
	Combination run	5 min (2 min)
	Football drills	5 min (2 min)
	Abdominal ball workout, core development, warm-down and static stretching	15 min total
WEDNESDAY	Active recovery, swimming, stretch	
THURSDAY	**SAQ session**	**40 min**
	Dynamic Flex with ball	15 min
	Power work with Jelly Balls	–
	Interval running	5 min (2 min)
	Football drills	5 min (2 min)
	Interval running	5 min (2 min)
	Football drills	5 min (2 min)
	Interval running	5 min (2 min)
	Football drills	5 min (2 min)
	Warm-down and static stretching	15 min total
FRIDAY	Personal weights, stretch, swim and sauna	
SATURDAY	**SAQ session**	
	Dynamic Flex with ball	15 min
	Power development including recovery	40 min (3 min)
	Football drills	40 min (3 min)
	Football-specific runs	30 min
	Warm-down, stretch and swim	15 min total + swim
SUNDAY Stretch – rest		

Repeat 14-day programme, reducing recovery times by 20 seconds in the first week and up to 30 seconds in the second week.

IN–SEASON: AMATEUR

7 - D A Y   C Y C L E

All sessions start with Dynamic Flex.

SUNDAY	Rejuvante/pool recovery	
MONDAY	**SAQ session** Team ball work Multi-sprints	90 min
TUESDAY	Personal strength and power programme	40 min
WEDNESDAY	**SAQ session** Team ball work Strength/power work	90 min
THURSDAY	Personal circuit conditioning	40 min
FRIDAY	Warm-up, light team ball work Rest	75 min
SATURDAY	Warm-up, **game**, warm-down, refuel	

References

Bennett, S. (1999) 'New Muscle Research Findings', Muscle Symposium, AIS, Canberra, Australia

Gallahue, D. L. and Cleland Donnelly, F. (2003) *Developmental Physical Education for All Youngsters*. Human Kinetics. New York

Gleim, G. W. and McHugh, M. P. (1997) 'Flexibility and Its Effects on Sports Injury and Performance', *Sports Medicine*, 24(5): 289–99

Hennessy, L. Dr (2000) 'Developing Explosive Power', Paper, SAQ Symposium, June 2000

Herbert, R. D. and Gabriel, M. (2002) 'Effects of stretching before or after exercising on muscle soreness and risk of injury: a systematic review', *The British Medical Journal*, 325: 468–70

Kokkonen, J., Nelson, A. G. and Cornwell, A. (1998) 'Acute muscle stretching inhibits maximal strength performance', *Research Quarterly for Exercise and Sport*, Vol 4, pp. 411–15

McMillian, D. J., Moore, J. H., Hatler, B. S. and Taylor, D. C. (2005) 'Dynamic Versus Static Stretching Warm Up: The Effect on Power and Agility Performance', *The British Medical Journal*, 39: 396

Oberg, B. (1993) 'Evaluation and improvement of strength in competitive athletes', in Harms-Ringdahl, K. (ed), *Muscle Strength* (pp. 167–85), Churchill Livingstone, Edinburgh

Page, P. and Ellenbecker T. S. (2003) *The Scientific and Clinical Application of Elastic Resistance*. Human Kinetics. New York

Pope, R. C. (1999) 'Skip the Warm-up', *New Scientist*, 18 Dec 164 (2214): 23

Rosenbaum, D. and Hennig, E. M. (1995) 'The influence of stretching and warm-up exercises on Achilles tendon reflex activity', *Journal of Sports Sciences*, 13: 481–90

Smith, L. L. et al (1993) 'The effects of static and ballistic stretching on DOMS and Creatin Kinase', *Research Quarterly for Exercise and Sport*, 64(1)L, 103–7

Smythe, R. (2000) 'Acts of Agility', *Training and Conditioning*, 5(4): 22–5

Sugden, D. A., Talbot, M., Utley, A., Vickerman, P., Thomas, N. and Cook, B. (1998) 'Physical Education for children with special educational needs', *Sports Council* Vol. 2

Walkley, J., Holland, B., Treolar, R. and Probyn-Smith, H. (1993) 'Fundamental motor skill proficiency of children', *ACHPER National Journal*, 40(3): 11–14

Whall, R. and Kellett, D. (2001) 'Time-Motion Analysis of the Football Goalkeeper', Research article; University of Liverpool

Glossary

Acceleration   Increasing velocity, specifically over the first 25 yards.

Aerobic   System that uses oxygen to release energy.

Agility   The ability to change body position quickly and accurately in any direction without losing balance.

Anaerobic   Energy systems that do not require oxygen to function; utilised during high-intensity exercise of a short duration.

ATP   Adenosine tri-phosphate: the only source of energy that muscle can utilise. All food gets broken down into this molecule.

Competitive skills   Skills such as running, jumping or lateral movements that can be used in the sporting environment.

Contrast   A stage after the resistance phase where the player/athlete performs the same drill but unresisted.

Dorsiflexion   Flexing the ankle by lifting the toes up as if you were trying to lift up a bucket with your toe.

Dynamic   Any movement, particularly a stretch, that actively moves a limb through its full range of motion.

Explosive movement   The ability to generate great amounts of force in a very short space of time.

Fast-twitch fibres   Present in larger proportions in explosive/power athletes, enabling them to perform explosive/powerful movements, as opposed to endurance athletes, who possess a greater number of slow-twitch fibres.

Flexibility   The ability to move a joint smoothly through its complete range of motion.

Force application   Ability to generate force from many small forces large enough to complete a specific movement or action, e.g. throwing a ball.

Goals   An important part of mental preparation in which the player decides and thinks about what he wants to achieve.

Hops   Single-leg repeated movements.

Jumps   Double-leg repeated movements.

Lactate   Leftover by-product of anaerobic metabolism that is converted back into ATP.

Maximum speed   Fastest speed achievable by an individual, usually achieved between 30 and 50 yards.

Muscular efficiency Utilising muscle energy stores in a manner that is not wasteful to the athlete. Achieved by minimising and eliminating unnecessary movements.

Neuromuscular recruitment Activities that work to activate more muscle units.

Peripheral vision Visual ability to see objects or movements at the 'edge' of vision, or while focusing on other objects.

Plantar flexion Pointing the toes downwards from the ankle. That is, full extension of the ankle.

Plyometrics Exercises, including hops, bounds and jumps, where maximum effort is expended while a muscle group is lengthening.

Power output The rate at which work is done.

Progressive overload In training, constantly forcing the body to adapt to new stresses.

Proprioception One's ability to adjust to any stimulus. This can be applied directly to or around the body.

PNF Proprioreceptive neuromuscular facilitation is a form of training that improves flexibility by increasing the strength of the agonist/primary muscle while decreasing the resistance of the antagonist.

Quickness The ability to generate a movement in a short amount of time.

Resistance A type of training that involves tools to increase the force required to initiate and sustain movement.

Specificity Training precisely for the demands of your sport or skill development.

Speed The ability to move fast over a specific distance.

Strength The ability to apply a force and overcome a resistance.

Velocity Speed of motion.

Index of drills

Adductors stretch 167
Agility runs – four-turn, four-angle run 90
  – swerve development runs 89
  – T-run 88
All defenders – cutting across your opponent 143
  – passing a cleared ball 142
Ankle flicks 8, 164
Arm mechanics – buttock bounces 47
  – mirror drills 46
  – partner drills 45
Arm roll and jog 5
Assisted resisted tow runs 116
Attacking midfielders – overspeed arc running 149
  – turn and attack 146

Balance beam walk 138
Ball drops 109
Ball placement decision-making 133
Break-away mirror 112
British bulldog 121

Calf stretch 168
Carioca 23, 163
Centre forward – vertical explosive heading power 152
Chair get-ups 99
Circle ball 122
Conditioning circuit 93
Combination runs 91

Dynamic visual acuity training 132

Endurance training – clock endurance runs 63–64
  – interval running sessions 65–67

Fast foot ladder – clock drill 83
  – combination drills – move and pass 78
  – crossover 76
  – forward step 74
  – giant crossover 80
  – 'Ipswich Town' grid 79
  – long pass 81
  – move and pass 77
  – pressing drill 82

  – single run 71
  – 'T' formation 75
Feel and distance 136
Feet–eye co-ordination development 86
Flexi-cord – buggy runs 100
  – lateral explosive first step development 102
  – out and back 101
  – overspeed 104
  – vertical power 103
Follow the thumb 130
Football-specific circuit 95
Forwards – cross and attack goal 151
  – peel off and turn 150

Goalkeeper – acceleration and jump drill 157
  – bunt bat drill 159
  – explosive diving 156
  – explosive ground reactions 158
  – fast hands 160
  – lateral speed development 155
  – narrowing the angles 154

Hamstring buttock flicks 22
Hamstring stretch 167
Hand weight drops 107
High knee-lift skip 12, 162
Hurdle walk 20, 165

Jog and hug 7
Jumping – multiple hops and jumps 56
  – single jumps 55

Knee-across skip 13, 162
Knee-out skip 15

Lateral running 14
Lateral speed development 113
Latissimus dorsi stretch 166
Let-goes 98
Lily pad drill 137
Line drills 84

Marker turns 125
Medicine ball (jelly ball) workout 114–115

Midfielders – assisted and resisted arcing 148
 – backward turn and cover 145
 – ball control, feed, turn, receive and shoot 147
 – Palmer drill 144
Mini-trampoline manipulations 139
Multi-player pressing drill 94

Odd one out 124

Pair drills – jockeying 28
 – lateral pair runs 27
Parachute running 108
Peripheral awareness 128
Plyometrics – drop jumps 119
 – low-impact quick jumps 117
 – plyometric circuit 118
Pre-turn 16

Quadriceps stretch 166
Quick box steps and jumps 85

Reaction ball 129
Robbing the nest 123
Running form – 1–2–3–lift 54
 – complex mechanics 61
 – curved angle run 60
 – hurdle mirror drills 59
 – lateral angled step development 53
 – lateral side-step development 52
 – leading leg run 50
 – pre-turn 49
 – quick side-step development 51

 – single dead-leg run 48
 – stride frequency and length 57
 – 'the square' complex mechanics 62
 – with a ball 58
Russian walk 17

Seated forward get-ups 97
Selection of sprints 29
Side lunge 19
Side-Stepper – jockeying in pairs 106
 – lateral runs 105
Single-knee dead-leg lift 11
Sled running 110
Small skips 9, 164
Speed endurance training – interval running sessions 68–69

Team combination runs 92
Tracking and focus 131

Visual acuity eye–hand reaction development 127
Visual enhancement training (VET) 134

Walking hamstring 21, 165
Walking lunge 18
Walking on the balls of the feet 6
Wall drills – knee across body 26
 – leg out and across the body 24
 – linear leg forward and back 25
W drill 111
Wide skips 10, 163
Wing back – attacking wing back drill 141

Also available

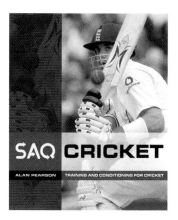

SAQ Cricket

Training and Conditioning for Cricket

ALAN PEARSON

With a controlled rotation of the body, the bowler fires the ball explosively down the wicket. Judging its flight with great precision, the batsman's lightning reactions see a shot played solidly towards the boundary. The fielder slides to collect the ball and, in what seems a single, graceful movement, gets to his feet and with great accuracy throws the ball directly at the stumps.

Featuring techniques that are tried and tested by leading coaches and players, this essential resource contains a wide range of clearly illustrated drills that provide a complete cricket training programme.

Available from all good bookshops and online. For more information on this and other A&C Black Sport & Fitness titles, please go to www.acblack.com

SAQ Tennis

Training and Conditioning for Tennis

ALAN PEARSON

Tennis is a dynamic, explosive sport that requires a wide range of skills – multi-directional speed, agility, hand–eye co-ordination and a high level of fitness. Featuring techniques developed over many years by some of the world's leading coaches and players, *SAQ Tennis* provides a complete conditioning programme that will help players at all levels improve their game.

Anyone who believes in helping players reach optimal fitness should have this book. I recommend it to all levels of the football world.

Graham Taylor OBE

Available from all good bookshops and online. For more information on this and other A&C Black Sport & Fitness titles, please go to www.acblack.com

SAQ Women's Soccer

Speed, Agility and Quickness for Soccer

ALAN PEARSON

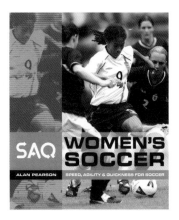

SAQ Women's Soccer details drills, programmes and soccer specific techniques that are guaranteed to improve multi-directional explosive speed, agility and acceleration in all conditions and environments.

SAQ Women's Soccer is an undoubted boost to the development of skilful female soccer players.

Sue Lopez MBE
Head of Women's Soccer,
Southampton FC

Available from all good bookshops and online. For more information on this and other A&C Black Sport & Fitness titles, please go to www.acblack.com

SAQ Youth

Performance and Movement for 12 –18-year-olds

ALAN PEARSON AND DAVID HAWKINS

Activity levels among children today are extremely low. Many young people do so little exercise that they are classified as 'inactive'. This leads to low energy levels, lack of concentration and a risk of health problems in later life.

SAQ Youth is a dynamic resource for young people, parents and teachers, designed to improve performance and participation in physical activity. Featuring an innovative conditioning and training programme which has revolutionised the world of sport, *SAQ Youth* is suitable for boys and girls of all abilities.

Available from all good bookshops and online. For more information on this and other A&C Black Sport & Fitness titles, please go to www.acblack.com

SAQ Juniors

Developing good movement skills for 4–11- year-olds

ALAN PEARSON AND DAVID HAWKINS

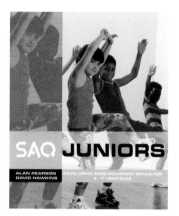

Activity levels among young children today are at worryingly low levels throughout the world. In the UK, one in three children between the ages of 2 and 7 do not achieve the recommended level of exercise – one hour a day.

Featuring an innovative conditioning and training structure, *SAQ Juniors* is suitable for children of all abilities and can be incorporated into existing physical education or used alone, under the guidance of coaches, teachers and parents.

SAQ training activities are providing new, enjoyable, achievable and challenging activities for children and their teachers.

Alan Duff
Physical Education advisory teacher
Durham LEA

Available from all good bookshops and online. For more information on this and other A&C Black Sport & Fitness titles, please go to www.acblack.com